To my beloved wife, Dorothy,
whose stedfast love, faithful support
and personal sacrifice
will always be gratefully appreciated

PREPARING
MISSIONARIES
FOR INTERCULTURAL
COMMUNICATION

PREPARING MISSIONARIES FOR INTERCULTURAL COMMUNICATION:
A Bi-cultural Approach

LYMAN E. REED

William Carey Library

1705 N. Sierra Bonita Ave.
Pasadena, California 91104

Published by
William Carey Library
1705 N. Sierra Bonita Ave.
P. O. Box 40129
Pasadena, California 91104

William Carey Library is pleased to present this book which
has been prepared from an author-edited and author-prepared
camera ready copy.

Library of Congress Cataloging in Publication Data

Reed, Lyman E.
   Preparing missionaries for intercultural communication.

   Bibliography: p.
   1. Missionaries--Training of--United States.
2. Intercultural communication. I. Title.
BV2092.U5R44   1984   266'.007   84-23060
ISBN 0-87808-438-X

PRINTED IN THE UNITED STATES OF AMERICA

Contents

Dedication *v*

Foreword *ix*

Preface *xi*

Introduction: Purpose and Scope *xv*

1. Understanding the Need 1

2. The Need for the Missionary to Understand the World 13

3. The Need to Understand Social Structures 33

4. The Need for Adequate Language Learning 59

5. The Need for Adequate Culture Learning 79

6. The Need to Understand the Importance of Worldview 99

7. The Need to Understand the Dynamics of Culture Change 119

8. Preparing Bicultural Missionaries 143

9. Understanding the Biblical/Theological Dimensions 163

10. Conclusions 181

Bibliography *187*

Index *201*

About the Author *205*

Foreword

We live in a tough world, and it is getting tougher. Its
cultural diversity is not only becoming more pronounced, but
more complex. Its economic disparities are generating more
polarization between rich and poor nations. And its political antagonisms are consequently more volatile. With each
passing year the majority of the world's peoples are feeling less secure and more fearful. Given this growing mood
of fear and insecurity it is not surprising that religious
inquiry is not diminishing but increasing. One might almost
say there has not been such a proliferation of cults and such
widespread religious huckstering since those troubled days
in the 1st century just prior to Pentecost.

Despite all the dark things one might say about the present state of the world, the Church has never been so busy
making Jesus Christ known, that He might be loved and served
among the nations. There have never been so many churches,
so many pastors and evangelists, and so many missionaries.
That is what makes this book so timely. It calls Christians
to devote particular attention to the most complicated of
all the Church's many teaching responsibilities, that of preparing her young people for **cross**-cultural missionary service.

This book was born out of years of faithful and fruitful
service in a most demanding Third World missionary situation.
Furthermore, it **reflects** the breadth of the author's personal training in three schools (Columbia Bible College, Wheaton
College, Fuller Theological Seminary). All three are noted

for their efforts to take the full measure of today's world
in order to responsibly train missionary and national church
leaders to be most relevant and effective in their service.
Finally, the insights of this book reflect broad and selective acquaintance with the best in current missiological
literature on this subject.

It has been my privilege over the years to know personally
Dr. Lyman E. Reed. I hold him in highest esteem. I have
rejoiced in his consistent discipleship under the rule of
Jesus Christ and his unwavering confidence in the integrity
of the Holy Scripture. Hence, when invited to write this
foreword I rejoiced over the opportunity it afforded me to
commend Dr. Reed and his work to the Christian public. My
prayer is that this book will be widely read and that it will
be used of God to shape the training of the growing numbers
of young people who in our day are deeply concerned that
where there are neither Christians nor churches there should
be both -- "holding forth the Word of life."

Arthur F. Glasser, Dean Emeritus
School of World Mission
Fuller Theological Seminary
Pasadena, California

Preface

In the past it has sometimes been assumed that missionaries are spiritual giants. They merely needed to be found, challenged, and thrust out into the harvest fields. While it is true spiritual values are very important, it is also true that missionaries need other kinds of preparation as well. There is a growing need for adequately prepared missionaries today. The missionary enterprise spans the globe. Mission boards and agencies are constantly recruiting additional workers. It is obvious that the need for training missionaries is ever with us. How well are we accomplishing this vital task?

It has been my privilege to serve as a field missionary for twelve years (North Thailand). Presently I have been serving as a professor of missions for fourteen years having a small part in the preparation of future missionaries. In the course of my research and preparation for classes it became apparent that there was a shortage of materials available showing how to go about preparing a missionary. Traditionally it has been accepted that Biblical and theological training was a necessity; consequently, many missionaries have had only this aspect stressed in their preparation for overseas ministry. Questions arose in my mind. Is there another ingredient that should be included in missionary preparation? Are missionaries being adequately prepared for their task? I sensed a shortage of materials available in this vital area of preparing servants of the King of Kings.

Out of this sense of need there arose a desire to produce a handbook to help fill this vacuum in the area of how
missionaries should be prepared. The focus of this volume
is aimed at the Bible college under-graduate who is concerned about serving Jesus Christ in a missionary vocation.
How to be prepared for cross-cultural ministry is my primary
concern. The task of missions is a complex one. Missionaries who cross cultural boundaries find themselves in peculiar and challenging circumstances in which they are expected to share the Good News of Jesus Christ. Such situations have prompted sincere questions on the part of new
missionaries shortly after their arrival on the field. Have
I really been prepared adequately for my task? Is there
something missing in my training for missionary service?

This volume is written from a thoroughly evangelical perspective. A firm commitment to the Bible as the Word of God,
and to a biblical theology of missions is hereby affirmed.
The writer is presently teaching in the area of Bible and
Missions and is firmly committed to the missionary mandate.

In addition to the biblical and theological approach in
the preparation of future missionaries the writer is convinced that an anthropological perspective is likewise essential. The insights from anthropology are valuable tools
in helping missionaries for their complex task ahead. In
no way does anthropology attempt to replace the ministry of
the Holy Spirit. Yet, the benefits of understanding culture,
social structure, and groupings of peoples are more and more
being recognized today. Missionaries are excited about the
clearer insights available to them through the behavioral
sciences. These helps are much needed in the cross-cultural
communication of the Good News.

Educationally we must integrate our biblical and theological knowledge with key insights provided by the behavioral sciences. Such an integration will better serve to
prepare the missionary to surmount the barriers to be faced
in cross-cultural communication. It is the writer's conviction that cultural anthropology and cross-cultural communication are essential elements in the preparation of a
missionary. Without such a background the missionary will
find his/her task much more difficult and even frustrating.

The missionary with a solid Biblical-theological background from an evangelical perspective, coupled with an anthropological and cross-cultural preparation, will feel
more adequately prepared for the vital task of missions in

the years ahead. From the educational viewpoint we must be preparing this type of missionary. The complex task of missions demands it. Our God will be glorified when His servants are prepared adequately to function effectively in cross-cultural contexts. The extreme importance of church planting and church growth warrants the best prepared missionaries possible.

Looking to the future, it is apparent that more and more missionaries will need and want this kind of training. Historically the Bible Institute/Bible College movement has provided a lion's share of the present missionary force. It is necessary to evaluate the adequacy of missionary preparation at this level. Where there are gaps in the curriculum new courses should be introduced. Cultural anthropology and cross-cultural communication courses are a must. For some schools it will mean up-dating their faculty qualifications to insure that these needs are met. In some cases new and better qualified instructors will need to be hired. Students will appreciate and benefit from such moves, and they will be more adequately prepared for missionary service.

Undoubtedly some questions will be raised. Will we sacrifice spiritual fervor for academic advances? Will the behavioral science insights supplant the ministry of the Holy Spirit? Such fears are unfounded, and they need not deter us from the task of preparing missionaries adequately for their vital task. Surely we must be anchored to the rock of God's Word and buttressed by solid evangelical theology. Yet, at the same time let's be alert to insights available to us from other sources. All truth is God's truth. We need to integrate it, and use it as the Holy Spirit guides us in preparing well trained missionaries to extend the Gospel "to the ends of the earth" (Acts 1:8).

Introduction: *Purpose and Scope*

What? Another book on missions? Yes, it is my desire
to produce a manual which will be helpful in understanding
how missionaries may be more adequately prepared for their
task of intercultural communication. While the primary emphasis in missionary training has been placed on the WORD
and WORKER, often there has been little or no stress placed
on understanding the WORLD in which we live and serve. This
is a matter for utmost concern in the preparation of cross-
cultural workers.

Young and inexperienced missionaries proceed into complex cultural situations and confront completely different
peoples among whom they are expected to share the Gospel
message. Without adequate preparation in cultural anthropology and principles of cross-cultural communication they
are subjected to severe culture shock, and sometimes failure to cope in the host culture. This practice has contri-
buted to missionary dropouts, and my concern is that something could be done to reduce that dropout rate by preparing better equipped missionaries in the future. It is true
that there are many variables when it comes to reasons for
missionary dropouts. Inadequate cross-cultural preparation
is one of them.

I propose to develop a bicultural approach applicable at
the undergraduate level. While it is true that some graduate schools and seminaries offer such training, many missionaries proceed to the ends of the earth without the benefits of graduate studies. More will be written regarding

the opportunities for continuing education in missiological
studies.

My primary aim is that this volume should be a basic
manual which will point the way toward becoming a bicultural
missionary. Hopefully this manual will be useful to the following groups:

1. Bible colleges, Bible institutes, graduate schools
   and seminaries which are preparing future missionaries.

2. Mission agencies which are preparing cross-cultural
   workers. This volume will be helpful for pre-field
   orientation for inter-cultural ministries at home or
   abroad.

3. Missions personnel currently on the field who are
   looking for ways to increase their effectiveness.
   This manual may stimulate further study when they
   return home on furlough.

4. Professional people who are preparing themselves for
   a "tentmaking" type missionary experience could benefit from this manual.

5. Young people anticipating summer missions or short
   term missionary involvement. This book will provide
   a cross-cultural orientation, reduce "culture shock",
   and prepare them for a more rewarding missionary experience.

6. "Third World" missionaries preparing to leave their
   own countries to share the Gospel in other cultures
   will appreciate the practical insights.

It is the author's prayer that this manual may become a
helpful tool in the preparation of future cross-cultural
workers. The unfinished task is great! The need for adequately prepared missionaries is even greater. Our Lord
has commanded: "Pray ye, therefore, the Lord of the harvest,
that He will send forth laborers into His harvest" (Matthew
9:38, NASB). It is only reasonable and proper that we
should insure that these workers be well trained and adequately prepared for cross-cultural communication.

Understanding the Need

The modern missionary movement continues to expand around
the world. The cry for missionaries is greater now that it
ever has been. Missionaries must be trained and equipped for
their task in order to serve effectively. The kind of training they receive needs to be evaluated and updated constantly.

THE NECESSITY FOR ADEQUATE PREPARATION OF MISSIONARIES

The preparation of missionaries is a vital aspect of the
missionary enterprise. The unique significance of the missionary's task points to the need for excellence in training.
A consideration of the Biblical imperatives and God's purposes in mission, plus the recognition of missionaries as
ambassadors of Christ will reveal the importance of an adequate preparation for missionary service. J. Herbert Kane
stated these emphases well when he wrote:

> The Christian mission is rooted in the Holy
> Scriptures. They and they alone are able to
> make man 'wise unto salvation' (II Tim. 3:16).
> From them we derive our message, our mandate,
> our motivation, and our methodology. Apart
> from the Word of God the missionary movement
> has neither meaning nor sanction (Kane 1974:85).

Biblical Imperatives

One of the clearest Biblical imperatives for missions

was pronounced by our Lord to His disciples and is recorded
in Luke 24:46-48:

> This is what is written: The Christ will suffer
> and rise again from the dead on the third day, and
> repentance and forgiveness of sins will be preached
> in his name to all nations, beginning at Jerusalem.
> You are witnesses of these things (NIV).

Our Lord Jesus Christ has commanded that the Good News--
"repentance and forgiveness of sins sould be preached in his
name to all nations. . ." The ministry of proclamation is
an essential part of the missionary task. Because of the
great significance of the message, Jesus said:

> Go therefore and make disciples of all na-
> tions, baptizing them in the name of the Father
> and of the Son and of the Holy Spirit, and
> teaching them to obey everything I have command-
> ed you. And surely I will be with you always,
> to the very end of the age (Matthew 28:19-20,
> NIV).

The life of the Apostle Paul exemplified obedience to
the Lord in carrying out the missionary task. His three
missionary journeys took him to Asia Minor and into Southern
Europe in evangelism and church planting. Thus, in writing
his epistle to the Roman church, he asked a series of pene-
trating questions:

> How, then, can they call on the one they have
> not believed in? And how can they believe in
> the one of whom they have not heard? And how can
> they hear without someone preaching to them? And
> how can they preach unless they are sent? As it
> is written, 'How beautiful are the feet of those
> who bring good news!' (Romans 10:14-15, NIV).

The commitment and concern expressed by the Apostle Paul
are forceful in reminding us of the extreme significance of
the missionary task.

God's Purposes in Mission

God's purposes in mission are revealed to us clearly in
His Word. Through the Prophet Isaiah speaking of the nation Israel we have a clear statement regarding the purpose
of God: ". . . I will give you as a light to the nations,

that my salvation may reach to the end of the earth" (Isaiah 49:6, RSV). The nations were included in the purpose of God as He provided salvation through the Messiah who was to come. During our Lord's ministry He declared plainly, "And I tell you that you are Peter, and on this rock I will build my church, and the gates of Hades will not overcome it" (Matthew 16:18, NIV).

Jesus was well aware of God's purpose in sending Him into the world. The cross was ever before Him, but He realized that as a result of His sacrifice God would bring into being a new organism: the church. As the Gospel was proclaimed, those who believed were added to His church. This continuing ministry of multiplying churches is an essential part of the missionary task. It was all a part of God's redemptive purpose for mankind.

Peter caught something of God's mercy and grace as he wrote: "The Lord is not slow in keeping his promise, as some understand slowness. He is patient with you, not wanting anyone to perish, but everyone to come to repentance" (II Peter 3:9, NIV). Here is a clear statement of God's missionary purpose. He is concerned that none should perish but that all should come to repentance. God, through His infinite love, has sent His Son to pay the price of man's redemption. The Apostle Paul grasped something of the greatness of that love when he wrote: "But God demonstrates his own love for us in this: While we were still sinners, Christ died for us" (Romans 5:8, NIV). In order for us to accomplish God's missionary purpose we must recognize the significance of the missionary task. This task will demand the finest of our Christian men and women, and well it should.

Missionaries as Ambassadors of Christ

Ambassadors of Christ must be well trained. In writing to the Corinthian church the Apostle Paul refers to ambassadors of Christ:

> All this is from God who reconciled us to himself through Christ and gave us the ministry of reconciliation: that God was reconciling the world to himself in Christ, not counting men's sins against them. And he has committed to us the message of reconciliation. We are therefore Christ's ambassadors, as though God were making His appeal through us. We

implore you on Christ's behalf: Be reconciled
to God" (II Corinthians 5:18-20, NIV).

Paul's analogy which likens God's servants to ambassadors is
a good one. Even as great nations send their ambassadors to
London, Paris, and Washington, so the Lord of the harvest
sends His ambassadors to represent Him among the nations of
the world. Since missionaries represent and serve the King
of Kings, they deserve the best preparation possible for His
service. The significance of the missionary task is great.
Because of the Biblical imperatives, God's purposes in mission, and because missionaries are Christ's ambassadors,
they deserve the finest training possible.

INADEQUATE MISSIONARY PREPARATION IN THE PAST

Reflecting upon the inadequate missionary preparation in
the past, we note certain areas of weakness which need to be
remedied.

The Weakness of the Monocultural Approach

Our Western tendency to be monocultural communicators is
one reason why we need better preparation for intercultural
communication. It is very easy for Western missionaries to
adopt an attitude that communicates the feeling that the way
we do things here at home is the right and proper way to do
so, whatever it may be. Donald Larson illustrates this tendency very well when he tells of a conversation with a short
term missionary.

>   I recently met a young man heading for a
> short term of missionary service in Southeast
> Asia and asked him what he was going to be doing
> there. He replied in all seriousness that he
> was 'going to teach the natives to farm.' I
> pressed him with a question: 'Don't they know
> how to farm there?' He thought for a moment and
> then replied, 'Well, I really don't know; I
> haven't got a very clear picture of things yet!'
> Imagine what the non-Christian of his adopted
> community would think of him if they should hear
> him say such things! Whether this young man
> knows it or not, these Asians were farmers long
> before the Pilgrims landed at Plymouth Rock and
> even long before there were Christians anywhere
> (1978:155).

In the past little attention was given to the receptor people and how to understand them as persons within their own cultural setting. As a result much of our own Western culture has been communicated along with the Gospel message. This has resulted in many nations thinking they had to become like Westerners in order to become Christians. Insights from the behavioral sciences, especially cultural anthropology, are a tremendous help in the training of contemporary missionaries. Grunlan and Mayers note:

> We have an imperative to present the gospel of Jesus Christ to all men. We have no imperative to present our culture to any man. Because we have learned the gospel within the wrappings of our own culture, we tend to assume that our culture is the biblical culture. It is important that we separate our culture from the gospel (1979:28).

In order for the missionary to become an effective communicator in a cross-cultural setting he/she must be trained to think and act biculturally. Since we tend to be monocultural in our prespective toward others, it is not automatic that we suddenly shift to bicultural thinking and acting when we move abroad. Nothing in our culture prepares us to function in another culture. There is, therefore, a need for adequate preparation before the missionary becomes involved in intercultural communication.

The Weakness of an Unbalanced Approach

Preparation for missionary service is a complex task. It requires a delicate balance of ingredients to produce a well trained missionary. Spiritual preparation of the candidate is vitally important. The simple yet profound facts concerning the new birth and assurance of salvation are essential aspects of that preparation. A good knowledge of the Word of God coupled with a keen spiritual outlook on life are likewise characteristics of a good missionary. Positive attitudes toward God and others were stressed by Harold Cook, professor of missions at Moody Bible Institute. In his missions classes he often stated:

> Students, the single most important area of your life and ministry will be in the realm of attitudes. It is here you will either succeed or fail as a missionary. Attitudes touch every nerve end of life. Your relationship to Christ, fellow

missionaries, national believers and non-
Christians will be deeply affected by proper
or improper attitudes (Parshall 1979:219).

In attempting to look back concerning how missionaries
were prepared in the past, perhaps this simple diagram will
be helpful (see Figure 1).

FIGURE 1

In the past the chief emphasis was placed on a cognitive
knowledge of the Biblical message, and a strong exhortation
concerning spiritual life--concerning the quiet time, the
deeper life, and the man/woman God uses. These emphases
were important, and they are still very important. We must
continue to stress these values and improve our methodologies
for communicating them. However, as Figure 1 indicates,
there is a vital ingredient that has been omitted in the
training of missionaries. The missing area is the WORLD!
Missionaries have not been trained to understand the world
around them; in fact, in many cases they have been sadly isolated from the outside world by ghetto-like institutions in
which they have been trained.

In 1973 *An American Directory of Schools and Colleges
Offering Missionary Courses* was published under the editor-
ship of Glenn Schwartz. This directory contains a listing of
133 schools, both undergraduate and graduate, which are offering missionary courses. Most of these schools are located in
the U.S.A., there are nine schools listed from Canada. Among
the 97 undergraduate schools listed, only about half offer any
courses in anthropology. It is possible that during the intervening years more of these schools have added anthropology
to their course offerings; nevertheless, there seems to be a

need for this emphasis in the training of missionaries (1973:xii-xxii).

Schwartz mentioned that traditionally missionaries were trained in two areas: (1) Biblical and spiritual knowledge; and (2) professional training (minister, teacher, doctor, nurse, builder, agriculturalist, translator, etc.). "But, as Louis Luzbetak, author of *Church and Cultures*, reminds us, missionaries were not trained to work cross-culturally" (1973:xxx). Schwartz proposes a triangle model for missionary preparation which looks like this: (see Figure 2).

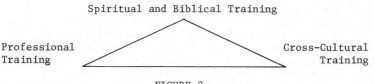

Spiritual and Biblical Training

Professional Training

Cross-Cultural Training

FIGURE 2

I agree most heartily with Schwartz's evaluation that "one of the most serious errors that missionaries make occurs when cross-cultural training is left out" (1973:xxxi).

Many missionaries were graduated from Bible institutes, Bible colleges, and seminaries that taught no anthropology and they proceeded to the mission fields of the world with a purely monocultural viewpoint. Some found it extremely difficult to adjust and to understand the cultures and people to whom they were sent. In some cases frustration led to nervous and mental breakdowns and consequent return to the homeland from which they had come. Their preparation for intercultural communication was inadequate. Such incidents point to the need for an adequate preparation for missionary service.

The Weakness in Ignoring Insights of the Behavioral Sciences

Evangelical Christians have been slow to recognize the value of insights gained from the behavioral sciences. For some strange reason, psychology, sociology, and anthropology were regarded as suspect; hence they were to be avoided. For some there has been an unfortunate confusion of behavioral sciences with the psychology of John B. Watson called

behaviorism. This was a psychological theory with roots in
the physical sciences and really has little relationship with
true behavioral sciences within the social sciences. Marvin
K. Mayers explains another aspect of the misunderstanding
regarding the behavioral sciences:

> The behavioral sciences study human behavior
> and then ask the questions of morality and ethics,
> of belief and practice. Many Christians have
> falsely assumed that since they have asked that
> question first they were putting man first, as
> do the so called 'humanists.' This assumption
> has produced a tragic misunderstanding and break-
> down of confidence in the fields covered by the
> behavioral sciences, including psychology, soci-
> ology, and anthropology, and other disciplines
> having a similar approach. The misunderstanding
> developed naturally, perhaps, since some be-
> havioral scientists follow this line of reasoning:
> Since human behavior is so obvious and so all-
> encompassing, there must be nothing more than
> that. Emile Durkheim suggested that all society
> is the interaction of human beings. This view-
> point allows no place for the supernatural.
> Durkheim's point of view does not receive uni-
> versal acceptance. A Christian can hold other
> fully acceptable views and receive the support
> of scholars in the field (1974:21).

Anthropology and missions ought to be congenial and
compatible bed-fellows; however, such a relationship has not
always been the case. Anthropology as an academic discipline
began about 130 years ago with the writings of E. B. Tylor.
Prior to this time anthropology was regarded as a sub-section
of theology, although, of course, this was not the discipline
we know today as cultural anthropology. With the passing of
years and the broadening of knowledge due to the changing
world situation cultural anthropology came into its own
following the abolition of slavery in England after 1830.

At this juncture there was a concern on the part of some
for the peoples of Africa and the effects of colonialism
upon them. There was a difference of opinion on how to go
about protecting the rights of African nationals. One fac-
tion, supported by many missionaries, wanted to give them
full privileges of Western civilization immediately. There
were others who wanted to study them before raising and protecting them. In this regard Paul Hiebert comments:

"Unfortunately, thereafter the missionaries and reformers
too often pursued programs of planned change without the
cultural contexts in which the change took place, while the
anthropologists too often proceeded to study the people with
little thought to how this knowledge could benefit the
people" (Smalley 1978:xxii).

Many of the earlier missionaries of the late nineteenth
and early twentieth centuries were concerned about the cultures and viewpoints of the people among whom they worked.
Yet, many were suspicious of the role of anthropology within
missions. After World War II there was a greater interaction
between anthropology and missions. The writings of Eugene
Nida of the American Bible Society became catalysts for
change. Nida published *Customs and Culture* in 1954, and
Message and Mission in 1960. Nida's two books and the
writings compiled in *Practical Anthropology* magazine all
played a leading role in strengthening this vital relationship. It has become more and more apparent that for the
training of missionaries today a basic knowledge of anthropology is essential in order to understand people cross-
culturally before proclaiming the Gospel message within their
cultural context. Even so, some professors of missions have
been reticent to see the value of the relationship of cultural anthropology to the missionary enterprise. Dr. J.
Herbert Kane in his book, *Understanding Christian Missions*,
states, "In our day the ideas of men are being substituted
for the Word of God. Anthropology and sociology are rapidly
replacing theology, with disastrous results. The vertical
dimension of the Christian mission has been lost and all
that remains is the horizontal" (1974:85). While Kane's primary reference may be pointing to conciliar theology within
the World Council of Churches, he seems to be a bit hasty
in his evaluation of the proper use of anthropology and
sociology in missions today. Some are fearful that the Holy
Spirit will be left out. Concerning this fear Grunlan and
Mayers comment:

> Cultural anthropology is not a cure-all
> for missions. It is just one tool of a well
> prepared missionary. Neither does cultural
> anthropology replace the Holy Spirit. No
> real missionary work takes place apart from
> the Holy Spirit. However, many Christians
> misunderstand the role and place cultural
> anthropology can have in effective ministry
> (1979:21).

I am in wholehearted agreement that anthropology is a vital ingredient in the preparation of future missionaries. Let's do away with misunderstandings, and steadfastly set ourselves to use the valuable insights from the behavioral sciences in the great task of missions around the world.

Our Weakness in Failing to Recognize a Fast Changing World

It is helpful and necessary to recognize that we are living in a fast-changing world. Great strides have been taken in the fields of technology, transportation, communication, and education, to name just a few areas. While it may have taken J. Hudson Taylor five or six months to reach China by ship in 1865, his great-grandson, James H. Taylor, the present General Director of the Overseas Missionary Fellowship (formerly China Inland Mission) s able to fly from Singapore headquarters to New York in less than twenty-four hours by 747 jet aircraft.

It is true that the message we have to proclaim is the same, but the context of the world around us has changed greatly. The preparation of missionaries must take into consideration the changing world in which we live and work. Reflecting on the Wheaton Congress on the Church's Worldwide Mission in April, 1966, Arthur F. Glasser was prompted to ask some pointed questions:

> Why do our training schools seem unaware of the fact they are preparing young people for service in a world that no longer actually exists? In these days of intellectual explosion, tremendous insight is being gained by experts in such disciplines as psychology, anthropology, sociology, management, personnel, and communications. Truth is truth wherever it is found, and regardless of who discovers it. At Wheaton we began to wonder why these insights and procedures were not being brought to the service of the church in its world wide mission? Why are they not being included in the general orientation of young people for overseas service? (1966:2).

Questions such as these have spurred Christians, particularly educators, to evaluate seriously how we train missionaries. A Roman Catholic anthropologist, Louis Luzbetak, asks a very relevant question in this regard: "Is it fair to send men out as missionaries without an adequate training in anthropology?" (1963:9). These are the kinds of questions which

need to be asked. As we become more and more aware of the
changing world around us with its explosion of knowledge in
so many directions, we shall recognize the need for better
preparation of missionaries. If we expect to accomplish the
great task our Lord has set before us, then we must grapple
with the issues relating to the training of our missionary
personnel. Alan Tippett has recognized the importance of
this task, and he has challenged the sending churches.

> The question for the sending church is therefore:
> Are you not responsible for sending out in the name
> of the Lord men who have more than just a devotion
> to duty and a missionary desire, if by your neglect
> of training them in the resources and facilities
> which are at your disposal, you leave them open
> to methodological and cultural errors, which can
> obstruct the work of God for the next century?
> I hold the home sending church responsible
> (1969:125).

These are strong words, to be sure, but we need to hear them.
We must give heed to this challange. Such an exhortation
simply points up the need for adequate preparation of missionaries in the future. The significance of the missionary
task demands it. Faithfulness to our Lord and His Great
Commission requires it!

Having noted the need for adequate preparation of missionaries, and having reflected briefly on how missionaries
have been prepared in the past, my task ahead is to set forth
the major areas which are important in training the missionary for intercultural communication.

$$\boxed{2}$$

The Need for the Missionary
to Understand the World

Since missionaries are destined to live and work in this
world, it is reasonable to expect them to understand the
world around them. The world is made up of lands, people,
and complex patterns of behavior. A common term that appears
frequently is the word culture. A missionary needs to understand the nature of culture, to develop an awareness of cultural divergence, to avoid misunderstandings and ethnocentrism
to formulate an attitude of mutual respect, and to recognize
the role of cultural anthropology in building bridges for
intercultural communication.

UNDERSTANDING THE NATURE OF CULTURE

What is culture anyway? How are we to understand it?
Hoebel suggests, "A culture is not a thing, nor is it a
precise entity. Nevertheless, it is conceived of as having
an existence and as being distinctive" (1972:53). This
approach may be helpful but is not especially clear or definitive. Robert Taylor writes that in popular terms "a culture
may be thought of as the way of life of a community or other
group" (1973:25). This is a helpful distinction in that a
way of life adds a realistic dimension.

Another analogy for culture is that of a flowing stream
in which mankind steps it and out, while the stream continues
on. "Yet, it transcends the individual; for the culture
according to which the individual lives existed before his
birth and continues after his death" (Hoebel 1972:53). How
then should we define culture? Anthropologists have agreed

basically on a definition of the term "culture." It has
been a long pilgrimage in the process of reaching consensus.
Keesing (1971:3-4) helps us to understand the efforts of anthropologists in defining culture by sharing the following
viewpoints:

> That complex whole which includes knowledge,
> belief, art, morals, law, custom, and any other
> capabilities and habits acquired by man as a
> member of society. - Tylor (1871)

> The sum total of the knowledge, attitudes
> and habitual behaviour patterns shared and
> transmitted by the members of a particular
> society. - Linton (1940)

> (All the) historically created designs for
> living, explicit and implicit, rational, irra-
> tional, and nonrational, which exist at any
> given time as potential guides for the be-
> havior of men. - Kluckhohn and Kelly (1945)

> The mass of learned and transmitted motor
> reactions, habits, techniques, ideas, and
> values--and the behavior they induce. - Kroeber
> (1948)

> Patterns, explicit and implicit, of and for
> behavior acquired and transmitted by symbols,
> constituting the distinctive achievement of
> human groups, including their embodiments in
> artifacts. - Kroeber and Kluckhohn (1952)

What are some of the characteristics of culture? It will
help us in defining "culture" to consider five basic characteristics of culture.

1. *Learned Behavior* -- Culture consists of behavior which is
learned. An individual does not inherit this particular
aspect of culture. It is true that a person is born into a
particular geographical and ecological setting. Some may be
born in Alaska, in southern Chile, or in the heart of Africa.
For each, the socio-cultural environment would be different.
Yet, the patterns of behavior a person learns come from
parental upbringing and interaction within a particular sociocultural setting.

A child learns a language from his parents and other family members. Whether he eats with his fingers, with chopsticks, or with knife, fork, and spoon is determined by these learned behavior patterns which are transmitted to each child born into that cultural setting. The process of learning one's cultural ways is known as enculturation. Concerning this process Hoebel states, "Enculturation encompasses all the processes by means of which the individual learns to internalize the norms of his culture" (1972:53).

2. *Shared* -- Culture is shared by a group of people. It is not just the peculiarities of one person's behavior. Culture is composed of many different patterns of behavior which are shared by the entire group. Some patterns of behavior may relate to the eating of food, the building of houses, the playing of games, or the care of the sick. Within a particular group all the members will be acquainted with the cultural ways which are acceptable to the group, and it is these values which are passed on by precept and example to each succeeding generation. This learned behavior is shared and transmitted by the group.

3. *Ideas* -- Another characteristic of culture is ideas. The faculties of the human mind come into play in determining what aspects of behavior will be practiced and how they will be carried out. Since man has been created with the capacity to think and reason, he is separate from the lower forms of animals. Hence, mankind has the potential for creating cultural ways. In regard to the idea realm Hiebert comments:

> In addition to patterns of behavior, culture is made up of systems of shared concepts by which people carve up their worlds, of beliefs by which they organize these concepts into rational schemes, and of values by which they set their goals and judge their actions. Viewed in this way, culture is the model that provides the people in a society with a description and an explanation of reality (1976:29).

4. *Cumulative and Changing* -- These patterns of behavior which are learned are also cumulative and changing. They add up during the course of many generations. Some types of actions are utilized more than others. Patterns of preparing food, eating food, dressing children, bathing and care of the body are all repetitive type actions. From time to time new behavioral patterns are introduced, and soon many people are practicing the new actions as well. Culture is constantly

changing as old ways are discarded and new ways are adopted and added to the familiar patterns already learned.

5. *A System* -- Cultural ways are wrapped up together into an integrated system. The basic building blocks of culture are composed of utterances, artifacts and actions. These areas are related to one another and they function like a system in every cultural group. Hiebert prefers to include the realm of ideas in place of utterances. He states, "Ideas, behavioral patterns, and material products are related to one another in cultural traits, and these are linked to each other in broader patterns called 'cultural configurations'" (1976:29-30). In this connection the concept of functionalism should be mentioned. This concept came into being in the field of cultural anthropology through the insights of men like Bronislaw Malinowski and A. R. Radcliffe-Brown.

> Beginning in the 1920's Malinowski vigourously attacked the tendency of some anthropologists to view cultures as little more than aggregations of unrelated traits, and he insisted on viewing them as systemic in nature. He emphasized the importance of explaining any cultural element in terms of its relationship to other system elements and its contribution to the operation of the system (Taylor 1973:46).

Culture, then, may be defined as learned behavior which is shared by a group. It begins with ideas which become customs as they are practiced. These patterns of behavior are cumulative and function as a system. It is imperative that missionaries try to understand as much as possible of the culture of the people among whom they live and work. The success of their work may hinge upon this understanding, or lack of understanding, of culture.

Often smaller social units, called subcultures, are found within larger cultures. "A subculture is a cluster of behavior patterns related to the general culture and yet at the same time distinguishable from it" (Grunlan & Mayers 1979:42). Our North American continent is composed of a unique mosaic of subcultures. A subculture is comprised of a group of people who share a common racial or ethnic heritage, a distinct language, customs, and cultural ways which are different in varying degrees from the majority of the population which surround them. In a sense they are a culture within a larger culture. Yet, they are distinct and recognizable by members of the subculture and identifiable as a separate group by

outsiders. A few illustrations of these would include the
Amish, Hutterites, Blacks, French Quebecers, and the various
North American Indian groups.

Society and culture may easily be confused. Hoebel reminds us not to confuse the two. "A society is people; a
population which occupies an identifiable space. The relations of its members are culturally patterned and distinct
from those of other societies, and its members are emotionally bonded by common linguistic and other forms of symbolic
representations" (1972:53). Culture, then, represents the
ways of life which different groups of people utilize as they
relate to the world around them and to other people. It is
important that missionaries understand the nature of culture
and how it differs from the term society.

Society refers basically to ways in which people group
themselves. Relationships of people to other people are
always important. Society has to do with the family, extended
family, schools, churches, clubs, labor unions, sports teams,
and the like. Some societal groups are linked by blood relationships, while others are linked by occupation or common
interests. There are societal groups which are based on sex.
For example, the Boy Scouts, the Rotary Club, and the Roman
Catholic priesthood are exclusively restricted to males, and
the Girl Scouts, Pioneer Girls, and the Daughters of the
American Revolution are composed only of females.

While society has more to do with groupings of people
and their relationships to each other, culture is the larger
arena in which people function. Cultural considerations
include geography, language, technology, economics, social
organization, legal systems, worldview, religion, and social
cultural change.

DEVELOPING AN AWARENESS OF CULTURAL DIVERGENCE

In our contemporary age of convenient transportation
which enables us to move from place to place around the globe,
we are made aware of groups which differ from one another in
their customs and life ways. But, with Robert Taylor we are
left with vexing questions "of whether boundaries between one
culture and another are detectable and, if so, how they can
be defined" (1973:49). Such questions have challenged anthropologists for decades. This is one facet that makes the
discipline of cultural anthropology so intriguing. "Anthropology is a study of universalities and uniqueness; a study
of startling contrast and surprising similarity; a study of

meaning and logic in what seems bizarre. It is a study of ourselves, as reflected in the many ways of life far different from our own" (Keesing 1971:3).

Cultural variability can be both startling and humorous at times. Roger Keesing recounts a pertinent illustration of this cultural divergence with reference to eating customs:

> A Bulgarian woman was serving dinner to a group of her American husband's friends, including an Asian student. After her guests had cleaned their plates, she asked if any would like a second helping: a Bulgarian hostess who let a guest go hungry would be disgraced. The Asian student accepted a second helping and then a third--as the hostess anxiously prepared another batch in the kitchen. Finally, in the midst of his fourth helping, the Asian student slumped to the floor; but better that, in his country, than to insult his hostess by refusing food that had been offered to him (1971:3)

Important drives within us as human beings motivate us to varying patterns of behavior. "Basic drives result from biological needs that must be met. All cultures provide means of satisfactory drive reduction by presenting patterns for goal achievement" (Hoebel 1972:53). Just how behavior will be patterned differs from place to place. Whether a person eats with chopsticks as Chinese and Japanese do, or with fingers as Northern Thai do, or with knife, fork and spoon as Europeans and North Americans do, has purely to do with the culture into which the individual is enculturated.

Now we can appreciate variance. It is a beautiful thing to be able to observe others who are different from ourselves and to appreciate them as they are. Such ability does not occur naturally; it must be learned. Missionaries must be trained to appreciate cultural variability.

What leads to this cultural divergence? There are many factors. Among them are the following:

1. *Writing* -- One important way cultures differ is whether or not the people have developed the art of writing. In this connection Taylor comments: "Cultures without writing are sometimes called nonliterate, a term some anthropologists prefer to primitive, as the latter term may imply inferiority or that the people are accurately representative of the

earliest human cultures" (1973:51). Nonliterate societies
are usually simple agrarian cultures with a way of life which
is quite different from contemporary Europe or North America.

2. *Urban or Peasant* -- Another factor which colors the cultural variability of a group is whether they live in an urban or peasant setting. Usually peasant societies are rural,
but they are located within the sphere of power of literate
civilizations and thus become dependent upon them. "The
culture of a peasant community, though influenced by and dependent upon the larger, more complex society of which it is
a part, remains relatively homogeneous and simple" (Taylor
1973:52).

Occasionally anthropologists have used the term civili- ᶜ⧸
zation. This is not synonymous for culture, but ordinarily
refers to cultures that manifest city life. The Yoruba of
Nigeria, for example, have population concentrations of over
100,000 consisting mostly of farmers. Yet, they are economically interdependent and are regarded more as an urban than
a peasant people.

3. *Ecological Factors* -- The basis for many types of cultural
diversity is provided by ecological factors. The natural
habitat where people live and the climatic conditions greatly
affect their cultural ways. It would be impossible for Eskimos of the arctic to construct igloos in Singapore which
is located near the equator. On the other hand, Malays would
experience considerable difficulty in finding bamboo for
housing in the frozen arctic regions.

Ecological factors also influence occupational pursuits.
Peoples who live near the oceans rely on fishing, whereas
peoples who are landlocked are often concerned with cattle
or sheep herding. The natural habitat greatly affects cultural variability.

4. *Biological Differences* -- As we travel to different lands
around the world, we note with interest the various racial
distinctions. Earlier anthropologists at first classified
mankind into three large families of races: the negroid, the
mongoloid, and the caucasian. However, contemporary anthropologists are of the opinion that there are numerous other
racial classifications instead of just three. E. A. Hooten,
for example, has devised a system of twenty-seven racial
categories (Taylor 1973:13). Likewise many other anthropologists have concluded that the old concept of "races" is use-
less scientifically. More consideration is being given to

the nature of ethnic groups. In this regard Hiebert comments
as follows:

> A great deal of anthropological reasoning
> rests on the assumption that cultures are sep-
> arate entities that can be clearly distinguished
> from one another, in other words, that sharp
> boundaries separate them. Moreover, a particu-
> lar culture is often associated with a particu-
> lar group or race of people and a particular
> language. It is becoming obvious that this is
> not always nor even usually the case, particu-
> larly in complex societies. One cannot make
> lists of cultural traits and determine from them
> the social or racial divisions within a society.
> It is important, therefore, to clarify how ethnic
> groups are defined and how they relate to one
> another (1976:276).

Some of the basic characteristics of ethnic groups are
ascribed status, consciousness of kind, shared values and
traits, and limited interaction among groups. Factors like
common ancestry or place of birth, common language, foods,
and religious beliefs are all integral parts of ethnic identity (Hiebert 1976:277).

The origins of biological diversity among the world's
peoples continue to challenge the minds of anthropologists.
Whereas the Bible affirms that God created man in His own
image, it does not explain in detail the origins of the diverse racial groups which exist. Thus, research continues to
find clues or possible explanations for this profound mystery.

5. *Demographic Factors* -- Demographics is the analysis of
population statistics. In large cities vast numbers of
people live and cooperate together. Their patterns of behavior are vastly different from life and activities in a
north Thailand tribal village consisting of eight or nine
houses. Small village life tends to be homogeneous and
simple, whereas big city life represents heterogeneity and
complexity. These factors naturally affect cultural divergence.

6. *Isolation and Contact* -- Another factor is that of isolation from other cultures. People who live deep in the forests
or jungles having little or no contact with the outside world
develop a pattern for living which is quite different from
the people who live in a city. Frequent contact with other

groups fosters culture change. This subject will be explored
later; however, it is helpful for missionaries to recognize
how these factors affect the people to whom they go with the
Gospel message.

AVOIDING MISUNDERSTANDINGS AND ETHNOCENTRISM

Communication across cultural barriers has the potential
for misunderstanding and distortion. In their eagerness to
serve the Lord missionaries have often blundered and been
ethnocentric in their relationships with people. It is
necessary for the missionary to know what ethnocentrism is,
what its dangers are, how to practice cultural relativism,
and how to overcome ethnocentrism.

What is Ethnocentrism?

Ethnocentrism is something which will always be with us.
According to Taylor, ethnocentrism "is defined as the practice
of viewing alien customs by applying the concepts and values
of one's own culture" (1973:64). In reality, it is viewing
other peoples' ways of life through our own colored glasses.
William Smalley offers an excellent personal illustration:
"It ranges from the repugnance my wife and I felt when our
Khmu houseboy ate a rat we caught in a trap to the uncontrol-
lable laughter that struck a Khmu friend when my wife cried
because our pet dog died" (1978:712). In Laos a dog is considered the scavenger of the village and is regarded as low-
est of the low. Hence, why shed tears over a mangy critter
like a dog?

The Dangers of Ethnocentrism

Chief among them are the areas of pride and an attitude
of superiority. It is not only missionaries who struggle
with problems related to ethnocentrism. As Bock suggests,
"Just as the student of a second language must struggle to
overcome his foreign accent, the anthropologist must struggle
to overcome his ethnocentric biases, many of which he is not
even aware of" (1974:380). It is very easy and natural to be
ethnocentric because "human beings are at the center of their
own perceptual worlds, resulting in a basic egocentrism in
which everything is judged in terms of the self" (Hiebert
1976:38). Thus, it is only natural for us to think that our
way of doing things is the right and proper way. Others
should do it the way we do, of course!

This attitude can be dangerous in that it destroys

personal relationships and sometimes other people too. To
those who are especially ethnocentric all other cultures
appear to be inferior. Consider the following case study as
an example and note the difficulties:

> On one occasion a group of Meo (Hmong)
> Christians were gathered for a short-term
> Bible School. Periods of Bible study were
> arranged. There were also times for recre-
> ation and for meals taken together as a large
> family. Some of the wives of the believers
> shared in the cooking.
>
> The local missionary who was doing some
> of the teaching, joined the Meo for a noon
> meal. They were all happily enjoying the
> food and conversation together until the
> missionary tasted one of the dishes and grim-
> aced openly, remarking in a loud voice, 'This
> food tastes flat. Didn't you put any onions
> in it?' A hush fell over the group and re-
> luctantly one of those working in the kitchen
> replied, 'Nzoe doesn't care for onions, so
> rather than offend him, the cooks refrained
> from putting onions in the food.' Nzoe was a
> gifted young Meo with a keen mind and a deep
> desire to follow the Lord. Although quiet
> and reserved as a person, he was faithful and
> well respected by his peers.
>
> When the missionary heard this explanation,
> he bristled and said loudly for all, including
> Nzoe to hear, 'Next time put in the onions. If
> Nzoe doesn't like it, he can go without. The
> rest of us want onions in the food.' A few
> daring glances were exchanged among the Meo,
> and then everyone went back to eating
> (Mayers 1974:317).

Practicing Cultural Relativism

One of the valued insights in anthropological literature
is cultural relativism. Earlier anthropologists regarded
cultural relativism as the doctrine that all cultures are
equally valid, although perhaps in different ways. Through
the years this value judgment has not been established by
scientific research; hence, the assumption of cultural
equality has been rejected. Yet, there is another aspect of

cultural relativism which is valid and useful as a tool to
promote understanding among cultures. "Cultural relativism
is most usefully understood as the practice of perceiving and
understanding any element or aspect of a culture by relating
it to its own cultural context" (Taylor 1973:64). Some would
prefer to call this concept cultural integrity.

If the missionary does not recognize the importance of
cultural relativism in the latter sense it is easy to lapse
into ethnocentric tendencies. As an example of ethnocentrism,
it is common for Americans to view Mexicans sitting in the
shade during the heat of the day, sombreros pulled down over
their eyes, and having a snooze, and to conclude that all
Mexicans are lazy. From the Mexican perspective, the nationals are merely enjoying an afternoon siesta which every Mexican knows is the only sensible thing to do during the heat of
the midday. The cultural glasses through which one looks will
determine the outcome of what has been perceived. Taylor reminds us that "ethnocentrism commonly leads to ethnic pride,
the belief that one's own customs are superior to those of
out-groups. Cultural relativism, properly applied, yields a
far more accurate understanding of the nature and functions
of alien ways" (1973:67).

How to Overcome Ethnocentrism

While it is true that ethnocentrism will always be with
us, we need not be discouraged and disheartened. There is
something we can do about it even though it is sometimes a
very painful business at times, as Keesing suggests:

> Becoming conscious of, and analytical about
> our own cultural glasses is a painful business.
> We do best by learning about other people's
> glasses. Although we can never take our glasses
> off to find out what the world is 'really like,'
> or try looking through anyone else's without
> ours on as well, we can at least learn a good
> deal about our own prescription (1971:21).

Part of the answer is to gain an understanding of another
culture in terms of its own values and assumptions, and then
we should begin to see its members as valid human beings.
Because we are bound by deep-seated attitudes and beliefs and
cultural differences are often very great, change seems to
come very slowly, if at all. Hiebert notes that, "For anthropologists, the history of their discipline has been one of
unearthing layers of ethnocentrism at the observational,

conceptual, and theoretical levels" (1976:39).

Yes, it is needful for the missionary to be aware of ethnocentrism and of its dangers related to the missionary
enterprise. The missionary can learn to work with and modify
his ethnocentrism, and anthropological tools will be very
helpful in the process. Smalley summarized it well when he
wrote:

> The value of an anthropological point of
> view, which sees customs and institutions in
> the light of the way they are worked out in
> many societies, is that it helps us to be aware
> of our ethnocentrism and to soften it. In a
> sense, the cross-cultural view which comes
> through the study of many peoples is an important
> aid in understanding the relationship between
> the cultural speck in our brother's eye as
> opposed to the log in our own (1978:712).

DEVELOPING AN ATTITUDE OF MUTUAL RESPECT

In order for a missionary to be effective as a servant of
Christ he must be able to develop an attitude of mutual respect toward the people and the culture on the field.
Smalley speaks to this necessity when he wrote: "Without
respect, without clear-eyed love, that identification which
is essential for the missionary will never be achieved"
(1978:713).

Building Trust

Part of the process of developing mutual respect will
revolve around building trust. Mayers calls it asking the
PQT--the prior question of trust. "Is what I am doing,
thinking, or saying building trust or is it undermining
trust?" (1974:32). It is necessary to check up on ourselves
regarding our attitudes and actions toward others. How do we
accept others who are different from ourselves? Do we perceive Blacks and darker skinned peoples to be inferior to
ourselves? How do we react in the presence of internationals
from a number of different countries? Smalley comments:

> We tend to respect what we like or learn
> to like. If we come from a background of advanced
> education, of emphasis on 'correctness' in our
> language, and on good breeding in our conduct,
> we tend to respect the high language and upper-

class characteristics of another civilization.
If we come from a lower stratum of American
society, we tend to be more at home with more
humble folk in a foreign culture. Full cultural
objectivity is impossible, but an awareness of
the vagaries of our selective ethnocentrism is
very helpful (1978:712).

Learning to Accept Others

Part of the missionary's preparation for cross-cultural
ministry should include learning to accept others who are
different. It is only natural for us to accept others who
look like, act like, and smell like we do. When we do this,
we also have the tendency to reject others who are different.
Some people are raised in communities where there are only
one kind of people. Consequently, such persons will have to
make a conscious effort to accept others who are different
and to learn some of their ways.

Leaving one's home community to attend school or work in
a heterogeneous society will expose one to cultural varia-
tions. Learning to make friends with those who are quite
different may well be a rewarding learning experience. It
will also help in developing trust relationships and in understanding others who are different.

It is not difficult for others to discern whether or not
the missionaries accept them as persons. Their attitudes
and actions soon give them away. Some missionaries have been
known to be extremely reticent to welcome nationals into
their homes. It is not long before the nationals begin to
realize that they are not welcome in the missionary's home.
At this point identification breaks down and communication
will also be affected. A barrier is in the way.

Some nationals overseas have noted that missionaries
have very little to do with them except for church and business matters. When the missionaries have a day off they
usually go off to associate with other missionaries or other
white business people. The nationals naturally conclude that
the missionaries do not want to develop informal associations
with them. They sense a lack of respect as persons and a sly
form of discrimination against themselves. Such attitudes
and actions soon build barriers between God's servants and
the people they desire to reach with the Good News.

Practicing Mutual Respect

Missionaries must be trained to respect others as persons even though they are different. They are not inferior or less valid--just different! Since all mankind is created in the image of God, we do well to practice respect toward others. We must be aware of our tendency to reject others, and replace that attitude with one of openness and acceptance. Developing mutual respect for others has the vital potential of rewards in building good interpersonal relationships. Such relationships will augur well for fruitfulness in missionary service. They will result in growing and rewarding ways of understanding people and the world around us. In this regard Mayers comments:

> Since mutual respect is a reciprocating relationship and must be carried on between at least two persons or groups, the persons or groups must stand on equal footing in terms of validity. One cannot force the other to do that which is untrue to himself. This means that both involved in a given relationship will learn, and both will change (1974:74).

Mutual respect needs to be practiced. Students in school may begin to cultivate good interpersonal relationships with other students who are different from themselves. If the school has international students, then the student has immediate built-in opportunities to practice mutual respect. In Christian service opportunities every effort should be made to respect and understand others who may be different ethnically, socially, or economically. While a student, courses like cultural anthropology, sociology, and principles of cross-cultural communication should be taken to broaden the perspective and to prepare the future missionary to be able to identify with persons of other cultures around the world.

THE ROLE OF CULTURAL ANTHROPOLOGY IN MISSIONS

In recent years the value of cultural anthropology for missions has been realized more and more. It is vital in four key areas: it helps in creating cultural awareness; it helps to build understanding; it helps in asking necessary questions; and, it helps as an aid to effective communication.

It Helps in Creating Cultural Awareness

A basic background in cultural anthropology will enable the missionary to be sensitive and culturally aware of other people and their needs. Cultural anthropology helps to provide the missionary with a holistic perspective concerning people and culture. There is a need for such a perspective as revealed by a mission executive reflecting on some areas of weakness seen in missionaries trained in Bible schools. Among these weaknesses were the following:

1. Lack of perception in separating out that which is the essence of the gospel and that which is cultural form of expression. Training that reinforces a middle-class role and suburban packaging of the faith. What is worse is that it is done uncritically and often unknowingly. For a missionary serving in a cross-cultural environment, this is critical.
2. Inability to integrate theory into real life. This is reinforced by the professor teaching theory but never risking himself in performance before the students out in the real world.
3. Lack of understanding of communicating the gospel in diverse environments. Personal work concept closely identified with witnessing to strangers, not to friends; comfortable witnessing to the world, but uncomfortable as friends with those in the world.
4. Lack of knowledge of the behavioral science skills and how they can be integrated with a Christian life and the missionary task. (Frizen 1972:45).

These are all areas where the prospective missionary needs to be culturally aware. Number four above is especially acute, because many Bible schools and colleges have not introduced courses in the behavioral sciences. More and more schools are becoming aware of this lack. Dr. Alan Tippett gives a personal testimony in this regard.

I should have kept a census of the many missionaries who have told me how they wished they had been trained in anthropology. I myself have often felt I could have reached that point of effectiveness in two years which took me ten as it was. In the end I had to

take extended furlough without pay to make
up the deficiency (1968:7-8).

There is no doubt that studies in cultural anthropology
are very useful in developing a sensitivity to people and to
cultural values. Missionaries who have obtained that perspective in their training are usually very grateful for the
cultural awareness which is so needful in their work.

It Helps to Build Understanding

Another way in which cultural anthropology may be of
assistance is in the area of building understanding. A missionary with a cultural awareness is in a much better position to understand people and potential problems. Cultural
anthropology helps the missionary to understand what makes a
culture click. What are the dynamics which hold a culture together? How are the people organized? Why do they do what
they do? These are basic areas which are foundational to an
understanding of people.

It is important how cultural ways are perceived and explained. In trying to interpret ethnographic data it is
helpful to distinguish between the "emic" and "etic" approaches. These terms were developed by a linguist, Dr.
Kenneth Pike (1954:8). An "emic" approach to culture views
it in terms of concepts and categories that are relevant and
meaningful to the nationals of a particular group. Both ex-
plicit and implicit aspects of culture are included. The
"etic" approach views a culture in terms of concepts and
categories which are described from an outsider's point of
view. An accurate understanding of cultural ways comes from
the nationals' viewpoint. The missionary, as an outsider,
may completely misunderstand and misinterpret the cultural
ways of a people. One cf the roles of cultural anthropology
is to help the missionary to recognize the importance of the
nature of culture. In this way better understanding is
facilitated.

The field missionary needs this kind of understanding.
Since the missionary works with people, he must seek to understand them and their cultural milieu. Otherwise his work will
be hindered and misunderstandings may result. How helpful it
is, as Nida observes, to be making an attempt "to see life
through the eyes of those who participate in it" (Smalley
1978:842).

It Helps in Asking Necessary Questions

The fact that missionaries work among peoples of various cultures inevitably leads to tensions arising and questions being asked. In seeking ways to relate to peoples of different cultures necessary questions must be asked. Cultural anthropology can be of great assistance in providing many of the answers. Tippet suggests some typical questions which arise for the missionary:

> What is the function of the social structure? What are the patterns of relationships in the family? Who marries whom and why? How do you explain the fatherhood of God in a matrilineal society? Do you demand of a pagan polygamist that he divorce his wives before baptizing him? Are the rites which honor the ancestor matters of reverence or worship? These and thousands of other questions are the stuff of anthropology, and whether we like it or not, they are also the burden of the missionary. Anthropology is certainly no substitute for ethics, but it examines all these things and asks why. What is the function? How do they meet the felt needs of the society? What are we doing when we change them? If we know and understand what is involved, we will be wiser by far in our thinking, our acting and our praying (1968:8-9).

Every missionary has questions after being involved in the work of the Lord for a few years. The questions arise naturally, but they are not always answered immediately. This may cause frustration and consternation for a season; however, it does challenge the missionary to think. This aspect is good. Missionaries are often led to ask, how can we communicate across cultures without a loss of meaning? Hiebert relates the field of anthropology to this enquiry:

> It is to answer questions such as these that some mission scholars have turned to anthropology and the other social sciences. In doing so, they do not deny the religious nature of human beings. But they recognize that people are also human: their bodies subject to physical and biological processes, their minds and spirits to psychological and sociocultural processes. And the social sciences are the study of these processes. So long as mission

involves human beings, these scholars contend,
an understanding of the social sciences can
help us to build more effective ministry
(Smalley 1978:xvi).

It is an Aid to Effective Communication

The missionary's chief aim is to communicate the Good
News of Jesus Christ and multiply churches composed of
faithful believers who are obedient to their Lord. He would
like to assume that the message is being understood clearly;
however, he may not realize, meanwhile, that there are cultural barriers standing in the way. This is one of the key
areas where insights from cultural anthropology may be of
great assistance. Nida was among the first to recognize this
key role for anthropology in missions:

> I would like to suggest that basically
> the study of anthropology provides a means of
> effective communication. In and of itself
> cultural anthropology does not provide the
> answers to how, when, and why certain ap-
> proaches should be made. But it can and
> should resolve some of the major problems
> of communication which are inherent in any
> missionary undertaking (Smalley 1978:840).

When missionaries are culturally aware of differences and
the distinction between form and meaning, communication will
be enhanced. If the missionaries are aware of the dangers of
ethnocentrism and recognize the value of cultural relativism,
their communication will be greatly improved. Some fall into
the trap of thinking that because we have learned the gospel
within the wrappings of our own culture, we therefore, assume
that our culture is the biblical culture. This approach will
hinder effective communication.

> It is only as we separate our own culture
> from the gospel and put it in terms of the
> other culture that we are able to communicate
> the gospel. Cultural anthropology gives us
> the conceptual tools with which to extract the
> biblical principles from their cultural forms
> and begin to make them applicable in any culture
> (Grunlan & Mayers 1979:28).

Utilizing the insights gained through cultural anthropology as tools in missionary work can be a rewarding experience.

Methodologies for evangelism may be developed when a clear
understanding of the people and their sociocultural milieu
has been gained. Strategies for church planting may be im-
plemented based upon effective research. In these ways the
fruits of cultural anthropology provide the means of effective communication. Nida advocates two benefits from anthropology and also adds a word of caution:

> The knowledge of cultural anthropology pro-
> vides an orientation as to (1) the relevance of
> the symbols by which the Good News is communicated,
> and (2) the means by which these symbols may be
> communicated in a context which is meaningful to
> the people of the target culture. Of course, a
> study of cultural anthropology will not guarantee
> that a message communicated to any group of
> people will be accepted. Far from it! Cultural
> anthropology only helps to guarantee that when
> the message is communicated, the people are
> more likely to understand (Smalley 1978:840-841).

Thus, in this chapter we have recognized the need for
missionaries to understand the world around them. The world
is vast, complex, and challenging. This motivates the missionary to be prayerful, patient, and persevering. By understanding the nature of culture, by developing an awareness
of cultural divergence, by avoiding misunderstandings and
ethnocentrism, by developing an attitude of mutual respect,
and by recognizing the unique role of cultural anthropology
in building bridges for intercultural communication it may
be seen that the missionary is in a much stronger position
to be an effective servant of Jesus Christ. Well prepared
missionaries led by the Holy Spirit are better communicators.

The Need to Understand
Social Structures

Our world is populated by numerous groups of people.
Each group represents a cultural heritage and is aware of
its distinctive identity. Since these groups are systemic
in nature, we can expect them to possess dynamics of social
structure and organization. For the missionary these considerations are important in the execution of evangelism and
church planting. Missionaries need to be acquainted with
the importance of social structure, status and role considerations, kinship relationships, group decision-making, rural-
urban factors, and in recognizing social structures as a
bridge toward church growth.

THE IMPORTANCE OF SOCIAL STRUCTURE

It is extremely important for the missionary to understand the social structure of the people to whom he goes with
the Gospel. Within the context of social structure lie the
seeds for potential growth and development of the church of
Jesus Christ. Eugene Nida notes a relationship between the
Gospel and social structure:

> The Great Commission and the history of
> Christendom both point clearly to the necessity
> of proclaiming the Good News, but neither in
> Scripture nor in the historical development of
> the church does the gospel include the details
> of social structure or church organization
> (1975:133).

Anthropological/Sociological Considerations

Every culture possesses a social structure, and it is important that the missionary be familiar with that structure. Sociology and anthropology provide the tools for gaining this understanding. Such insights will become aids not only for understanding the people but also for the development and multiplication of future churches. Donald McGavran is one who has researched and popularized this approach.

> Sociological/anthropological situations are exceedingly important if we are to comprehend the ability of congregations and denominations to flourish on new ground, reproduce themselves, communicate the Christian faith, and influence their nation. It is desirable, therefore, to understand the church as it advances into new areas along the lines also of these sociological/ anthropological characteristics. They add a depth of comprehension which remains hidden if we employ only ecclesiastical or theological frames of reference (1979:2).

The research and writings of anthropologists and field missionaries have revealed helpful principles which are so essestial for effective missionary work. Let's try to understand some of the dynamics of social structure.

Basic Components of Social Structure

McGavran has identified eight components of social structure:

1. *The unique self image.* The way in which a cultural system fits together provides a self image for that group. Their social structure reveals certain characteristics of a unique self image.

2. *Marriage customs.* These are always a very important aspect of any group. Some cultures have a clear and strict code of ethics when it comes to who marries whom. Often the parents play a leading role in arranging marriages in many cultures.

3. *The elite or power structures.* Every group has a segment of the whole whom they regard as the elite or as those who possess great influence. Often leadership is elected or appointed from among this elite group. The way in which this political organization functions is very important to the social structure of the group.

4. *Land rights*. Who owns the land and how much land is owned become key factors in determining social structure. In some cases a dozen key families may own or control 75-90 per cent of the land. This fact strongly affects the relationships with others in the group.

5. *Sex mores*. The guidelines or lack of them concerning sexual behavior are important aspects in understanding the social structure of a group. Each group possesses a certain set of values in this regard and these are taught to the younger generation as they approach adulthood. Such values are important for interpersonal relationships.

6. *People consciousness*. Every group possesses a capacity to recognize itself as a distinct group. Sometimes certain types of dress or ornaments become outward indicators of their people consciousness. Other nearby groups will recognize these symbols as indicators of that particular group. It is here that language plays a leading role.

7. *Geographic location*. In many cultures the location of a family's home is determined by their place within the social structure. Those who are wealthy and prestigious live in an area which is known to be the location of important and influential people. Prestige also accrues from this practice as well.

8. *Language*. Nothing is more distinctive of a people than their language. Within a nation where there are many sub-groupings there may be a ranking of languages. A national language may be designated, and all other languages used are automatically less prestigious than the national language. Nevertheless, the language a group speaks is very important to the integrity and solidarity of that group (1970:183-193).

Seeing Holistically

The longer a missionary studies the social structure of a people the more he/she will be convinced of the interrelationships within a cultural system. Anthropology contributes to a knowledge of ourselves and others. Nida summarizes three outstanding insights in relation to social structure:

1. The behavior of a people is not haphazard, but conforms to a pattern.
2. The parts of the pattern of behavior are interrelated.

3. The life of a people may be oriented in
   many different directions (1975:52-53).

These considerations will point to the holistic view of a
group and their culture. Examination of the social structure
of a group will reveal this holistic perspective. As the
missionary communicates the Good News this holistic aspect
will need to be kept in view.

Social Structure and Communication

When it comes to communicating the Gospel the significance
of social structure is very helpful. Nida has noted two obser-
vations which are vital for good communication:

> (1) people communicate more with people of
> their own class; that is, interpersonal commun-
> ication of a reciprocal nature is essentially
> horizontal, and (2) prestigeful communication
> descends from the upper classes to the lower
> classes, and this vertical communication is pri-
> marily in one direction and tends to be princi-
> pally between adjacent groups (1960:99).

The missionary must not overlook the social structure of a
group. This structure provides keys to communication which
must be employed. Nida advocates three key principles of
communication relating to social structure:

1. Changes in social structure may alter the
   religious view of behavior.
2. Effective communication follows the patterns
   of social structure.
3. A relevant witness will incorporate valid
   indigenous social structures (1960:132-133).

STATUS AND ROLE CONSIDERATIONS

One key aspect of social structure has to do with status
and role relationships. This is a meaningful area for the
missionary to understand in his personal interrelationships
with people in a cross-cultural context.

Status Defined

A careful understanding of status and role factors will
enable the missionary to understand the cultural system and
be better able to work within it. In simple terms, "a status

is a position or place in a social system and its attendant
rights. Status defines a place in a social system" (Grunlan
& Mayers 1979:135). Status within a group helps people to
understand their relationships to others in the group.
Taylor explains its function in a helpful way.

> A status is probably most usefully under-
> stood as a label that identifies some kind of
> group member, used either by a participant or
> an outside observer. The status is some aspect
> of some kind of person's relationship with an-
> other kind of person, useful for identifying
> the total set of relationships one has with
> the other (1973:244).

Each person within a group has a certain degree of status.
Persons within a group perceive themselves as having a certain amount of status in relation to others within the group.
One person may be a father, another a son, another a widow,
another a mother, and still another a daughter. These
terms denote status which is understood by the group.
Hiebert sums up nicely when he writes:

> Taken together, the statuses in a society
> provide it with a 'social structure,' a frame-
> work into which people are socially placed.
> Moreover, meanings and values are assigned to
> these statuses. The roles associated with
> them allow people in different statuses to
> interact smoothly and in predictable ways
> (1976:144).

Types of Status

Anthropologists and sociologists commonly speak of two
kinds of status: ascribed status and achieved status. "An
ascribed status is one which a society assigns to an individual, usually based on characteristics of birth such as
sex, age, race, or ethnic groups, and social class"
(Grunlan & Mayers 1979:137). In some societies there are
those who have inherited wealth and with it comes a degree
of status. "Primogeniture refers to a system of inheritance
in which the family's wealth and position pass to the first-
born son" (Grunlan & Mayers 1979:138).

Social class is also a determiner of status. This is
usually reckoned on the basis of wealth, occupation, and
position in society. Race and ethnic groups are also status

determiners. There are always those who perceive of themselves as being superior or higher than other groups ethnically. This easily leads to racism which is sin, but this
racial superiority is fostered and communicated by a particular group in order to maintain its distinctiveness and integrity. Ascribed status distinctions, which are foundations
of human social structure, are based upon age, sex, the pre-
marital state, childbearing, and kinship.

Achieved status is that which can be gained by persons
within their cultural system. Education, social striving,
and a good occupation are important factors in obtaining
achieved status. Hoebel observes:

> Cultures that emphasize achievable status
> are marked by internal social mobility, social
> striving, and (on the whole) competitiveness
> and individualism. Emphasis is placed upon
> fulfillment of self and assertiveness. The
> social gain is ideally a greater ultimate
> efficiency because capable persons are not
> barred from effective performance in those
> capacities for which they have adequate apti-
> tudes. Conversely, caste and rigid class
> systems are socially wasteful because they
> ascribe roles to people who are not necessar-
> ily well suited to their performance, while
> at the same time they bar potential adepts
> (1972:363-364).

Roles

The role a person plays in society is very closely associated with his/her status. "Role is the behavior, attitudes,
and values associated with a particular status . . . role is
a blueprint for the behavior associated with a status"
(Grunlan & Mayers 1979:136). Persons often fulfill more
than one role at a time. For instance, it is possible for a
man to be a husband, a father, a son, a teacher, a friend, a
graduate student, and many other statuses at the same time.
The behavior and responsibilities pertaining to each role
would be different.

Social roles make up the warp and woof of cultural ways
and interpersonal relationships within a society. Bock
explains it this way:

Most social roles have among their attributes one particular kind of attribute called the role label. Role labels, together with distinctive uniforms and other types of insignia, help both the members of a society and ethnographers to recognize which roles are being performed. The label is a word or phrase used by members of a society to address or refer to a particular kind of person (1974:93).

Persons within a society are taught their roles by the adult members of the group and they are expected to function according to those prescribed roles. Hoebel refers to this aspect when he writes: "Social behavior is the behavior of persons performing their appropriate roles according to the statuses which have been ascribed to them or which they have achieved by mastery of the roles" (1972:374).

Status and Role Confusion

Roles will vary from culture to culture; hence, the missionary will need to be careful in understanding the various roles in the culture where he lives and serves. "Much of the confusion of moving from one culture to another arises from a misunderstanding of behavioral ideals and patterns of the new culture" (Hiebert 1976:153). How is a missionary perceived by a society where they have never seen a missionary? Jacob Loewen shares an illustration of how missionaries are perceived in parts of Latin America:

In most South American societies which we have been able to observe, the white man is not unknown. But the white men of their experience have consistently filled a narrow range of roles--usually that of *patron* 'feudal master,' or colonial police officer. It is most normal, therefore, to also classify the missionary in one or the other or both of these categories. In fact, it is our feeling that most missionaries to tribal societies in South America have been stereotyped by the people into these categories, and this usually not entirely without reason (1975:436).

Confusion may result when the missionary, as an outsider, attempts to play a role that doesn't exist in the new culture. If the people have never seen or heard of a missionary, they find it difficult to know what role expectations are appropriate for the strange white man. This may cause doubts and suspicions until they are able to assign a status and a commensurate role for the missionary. In this connection Hiebert cautions, "It is important, therefore, that an outsider choose a role understood by the people or, at least, be aware of the role in which they have cast him. To fail to do so can create continual misunderstandings and possible rejection" (1976:153-154). The missionary may have a clearer definition of status and role for himself, but the cross-cultural understanding of them by the nationals may be quite different.

KINSHIP RELATIONSHIPS

The age-old axiom, "blood runs thicker than water," certainly emphasizes the importance of kinship relationships. Family and blood ties are regarded as being very important by peoples all over the world. For some it is more true than for others. Aspects of kinship are universal and they need to be understood by the missionary in his work.

Their Universality

Kinship relationships are found in societies all over the world. Murdoch notes, "Kinship systems constitute one of the universals of human culture. The author is not aware of any society, however primitive or decadent, that does not recognize a system of culturally patterned relationships between kinsmen" (1949:3). Anthropologists have become aware of a great variety of kinship systems. Every society has some organized form of relating one person to another within its group. North Americans often place a lesser value on kinship relationships than do other groups in parts of the world where one's family members are considered of great significance.

Their Importance

Kinship systems provide a sense of cohesion and group awareness which is vital to the functioning of any group. It is important for missionaries to understand these relationships. "It is a hard fact; however, that it is simply impossible to understand the workings of most societies without grasping their approach to kinship--kinship systems, kinship functions, kinship terms" (Hoebel 1972:441). The family tie does not end with parents and children. Kinship extends to include grandparents, uncles, aunts, brothers, sisters, and cousins as well. Among many societies these

relationships are regarded as vital and very important in
the functioning of social organization. In some groups, for
instance, an uncle on the mother's side plays the role of
disciplining a child instead of the child's father. "In all
societies, the cementing effect of these bonds is strong
enough to produce a network of special relations between relatives that makes the relationship group distinguishable as
an entity within the larger society" (Hoebel 1972:441-442).

Extended Family

The nuclear family--composed of a husband and a wife and
their children--is the best known and almost universal human
social grouping. Families may be more complex in some societies. According to Murdoch, "An extended family consists
of two or more nuclear families affiliated through an extension of the parent-child relationship rather than of the
husband-wife relationship; i.e., by joining the nuclear family of a married adult to that of his parents" (1949:2).

In some instances several sons will bring their wives
home to live with the husband's parents. This may be a temporary arrangement, or it may last for many years. As these
younger families bear and rear their children the extended
family continues to grow. Often other relatives, uncles,
aunts, and cousins will live nearby in the same village. In
this way it may be seen that extended family relationships
are very strong, and they need to be understood by the missionary who comes in as an outsider and enters the kinship
system of small village life. Hoebel draws attention to the
universal functions of the family:

> (1) The institutionalization of mating and
> the establishment of legal parents for a woman's
> children. (2) Nurture and enculturation of the
> young. (3) Organization of a complementary
> division of labor between spouses. (4) The
> establishment of relationships of descent and
> affinity (1972:439).

GROUP DECISION-MAKING

From our North American perspective it is natural for us
to think of religious commitment as an individual matter.
This is typical ethnocentric thinking. For many peoples of
the world such commitments are only made through group decision-making processes. This is another aspect of social
structure which the missionary needs to understand.

Group Solidarity

Understanding the social structures of a people will enable the missionary to work with the system rather than
against it. The solidarity of the group should be preserved
in order to achieve the best results. Tippett explains the
dynamics involved with group orientation:

> Biblically the church is concerned in the
> same terms as a body. The total group is really
> the decision-making body, although it may be for
> one individual to make the pronouncement as the
> representative of all. In many communal socie-
> ties there is no decision without unanimity in
> the village or tribal councils. The decision-
> making group may be a family, or a village, or
> a lineage, or a caste. This is a basic determinant
> in people movements. The bulk of the church in
> the Pacific has been won by people movements;
> that is, not isolated individuals, but by indi-
> viduals acting within their own social patterns
> and by means of their own decision-making
> mechanisms. Thus the total structures have
> been won (1971:200-201).

This approach does not destroy families, but binds them together as they jointly decide for Christ. Churches may be
established without a great deal of social upheaval; thus,
solidarity of the group is preserved. There is also greater
potential for church growth.

Tippett refers to Jesus' ministry in Sychar of Samaria
where He conversed with the woman at the well. The account
is recorded in the fourth chapter of the Gospel of John.

> ° Jesus saw the potential in the situation,
> for the winning of a group as a group. It had
> to be this way; where would an isolated Samari-
> tan have stood in Jewish or Samaritan society
> as a follower of Jesus? There had to be a
> multi-individual unit, a fellowship. Jesus
> recognized the possibility in the situation,
> pointed out to the disciples that the fields
> were ripe unto harvest (John 4:35), and He
> moved in across cultural barriers for an in-
> gathering (1971:208).

McGavran likewise, in agreement with Tippett, speaks of

people movements to Christ as "multi-individual, mutually interdependent conversion." He explains the process in this manner:

> What I am affirming is that conversion does not have to be by the decision of a solitary individual taken in the face of family disapproval. On the contrary, it is better conversion when it is the decision of many individuals taken in mutual affection. Multi-individual means that many people participate in the act. Each individual makes up his mind. He hears about Jesus Christ. He debates with himself and others whether it is a good thing to become a Christian. He believes or does not believe. If he believes, he joins those who are becoming Christians (1980:340).

The aspect of being "mutually interdependent means that all those making the decision are intimately known to each other and take the step in view of what the other is going to do" (McGavran 1980:340). Of course, when such multi-individual conversion takes place, there is immediate need for sound teaching of the Word of God in order that these believers may be established in the Christian faith and not be drawn back into the old religious ways. In places where illiteracy is high this process of teaching and nurturing will be more time consuming; nevertheless, it is vitally necessary.

Advantages of Group Decisions

Using the approach of group decision-making the missionary works within the social structure of the people. This is what they understand and appreciate.

> Instead of a **conglomerate of conv**erts from many different backgrounds who must learn to get along together, people movement congregations are comprised of one kind of people accustomed to working and living together. People-movement churches are therefore more stable, less dependent on mission and missionary and more likely to bear up well under persecution. Conviction is buttressed by social cohesion (McGavran 1980:337).

Social solidarity within the group is maintained and this provides an excellent foundation for greater church growth. In his book, *Bridges of God*, Donald McGavran reflects on the significance of people movements in India. He suggests that people movements have five considerable advantages:

1. They have provided the Christian movement with permanent Christian churches rooted in the soil of hundreds of thousands of villages.
2. With them the spontaneous expansion of the Church is natural.
3. They have the advantage of being naturally indigenous.
4. Spontaneous expansion involves a full trust in the Holy Spirit and a recognition that the ecclesiastical traditions of the older churches are not necessarily useful to the younger churches arising out of the missions from the West.
5. New groups of converts are expected to multiply themselves in the same way as did the new groups of converts who were the early churches (1955:87-88).

Whereas group decision-making has advantages for solidarity and church growth it may also produce some problems. First, there may be many in the group who give mutual assent to faith in Jesus Christ, but in reality do not express saving faith. This practice produces nominalism which is not conducive to spiritual vitality or potential church growth.

Walter L. Liefeld, a participant in the March, 1976, Trinity Consultation on Theology and Mission, sponsored by Trinity Evangelical Divinity School, shared a word of caution regarding multitudes turning to the Lord Jesus Christ in our day. He suggests that some observers have been skeptical for two reasons: "One is the fear that the emphasis on numbers may lead us to accept as converts those who have not been genuinely regenerated. The other is a pessimism based on the assumption that the end of the present age will find few, rather than many, true believers on earth" (Hesselgrave (Ed.) 1978:180). Such a criticism is understandable and similar reactions have been voiced by others.

Secondly, when large numbers of a group turn to Christ all at once, the tremendous task of discipling and teaching them is overwhelming. If they are not taught promptly, it is natural for them to be tempted back into the old familiar ways which they know so well. On the other hand, some missionaries would welcome the challenge of teaching hundreds or thousands as opposed to no one or very few turning to Christ.

Thirdly, there is the danger that when large numbers turn to Christ in a people movement there are some who take the step just because their family members did so; hence, they do not yet fully understand the Christian message or the significance of the new birth. Faithful preaching and teaching of the Word of God in the national language may well correct such a situation.

URBAN-RURAL FACTORS

Whether people live in country areas or in small or large cities affects social structure as well. Missionaries should be aware of the dynamics of urban-rural considerations for they do have a bearing on the acceptance of the Christian message.

Redfield's Continuum

The anthropologist, Robert Redfield, developed an approach to help understand people and their cultural setting. He set up a continuum with strongly folk cultures at one end and strongly urban ones at the other end. His idea was to examine a group of people and attempt to place them on the continuum as being primarily folk or urban in their basic orientation. This is helpful for classification purposes.

Non-literate peoples would naturally fall toward the folk end of the continuum. Concerning them Taylor comments:

> Non-literate cultures, which would include those with band, tribal, and chiefdom levels of integration, fall near the folk end of the continuum. A folk community is small, and its members have few contacts with outsiders. Its culture is homogeneous . . . The people are bound together largely by kinship ties, which are usually rather extensive. Technology is relatively simple and economic exchange is limited. Tradition rules--the people do not reflect upon or question their well-integrated culture (1973: 55).

Groups of this nature display a strong sense of cohesiveness. New ideas are accepted only with great caution; thus, the missionary needs to know the cultural milieu before

proclaiming the Gospel. Nida draws attention to two main
types of face-to-face societies: folk and primitive.

> The first is a dependent type of society
> which looks toward the urban center, derives
> considerable benefit from it, and also con-
> tributes much to it, especially by way of raw
> materials. The primitive society, on the other
> hand, is also a strictly face-to-face grouping,
> whether loosely or tightly organized, but its
> economy and orientation are almost completely
> independent of outside influences (1960:107).

People who live in urban settings are quite different
from rural peoples as regards their sociocultural environment. The large cities around the world are growing by
leaps and bounds. Hesselgrave suggests, "By 1990 more than
half of the world's population will probably live in cities
of one hundred thousand people or more. Moreover, the
swiftest pace of urban growth has shifted from advanced
nations to the less developed nations as those of South
America and Africa" (1978:366).

Rural peoples are moving into the cities by the thousands looking for work and a better way of life. The
cities draw them like a huge magnet. In citing an illustration from modern India, McGavran contrasted life in the
city with life in the rural areas:

> The city is where almost all bishops live,
> where all seminary professors live, where all
> editors of Christian magazines live, where all
> great gatherings are held, where conference,
> synod, and presbytery headquarters are found.
> The churches are lighted with electricity and
> cooled with ceiling fans. Well-dressed men
> and women come to them on bicycles or in rick-
> shaws or cars. Yet probably less than one
> quarter of all Christians in India (perhaps
> four million of them) live in towns and cities,
> while three quarters live in villages where no
> seminaries, no colleges, and no hospitals exist,
> and where the Word of God is still read in the
> evening by lantern light (1979:35).

RECOGNIZING SOCIAL STRUCTURE AS A BRIDGE TO CHURCH GROWTH

Having noted the importance of and some of the elements
of social structure, missionaries should recognize how these
factors may be helpful as bridges to future church growth.
Working within the social structure and understanding its
dynamics will prove to be positive assets to successful missionary endeavor. Related factors like the significance of
the homogeneous unit principle, soil testing, and the resistance-receptivity axis need to be understood by the missionary.

The Homogeneous Unit Principle

Group consciousness is very much a part of culture around
the world. Any group of people is quick to point out those
of their own kind and those who are different. Donald
McGavran has introduced his oft-quoted axiom, "People like to
become Christians without crossing racial, linguistic, or
class barriers" (1980:223). There is nothing unusually in-
tellectual about this observation. It is a perfectly natural
phenomenon which we see in operation day in and day out. There
are biblical foundations for this understanding. McGavran has
aptly pointed out that,

> Nineteen hundred years ago the Church found
> that the Jews liked to become Christians without
> crossing racial barriers. The Jewish caste was
> a tightly knit society. It had effective control.
> It insisted that Jews marry Jews. All this pro-
> vided a broad avenue for the expansion of a Jew-
> ish church. As long as Jews could become Chris-
> tians within Judaism, the Church could and did
> grow amazingly among Jews, filling Jerusalem,
> Judea, and Galilee (1980:230-231).

In the United States there has been a concerted effort
to integrate white churches with Blacks and other ethnic
minorities. There has not been a great deal of success in
this endeavor. In fact, Wagner states: "Many people have
observed, for example, that American churches that mix Blacks
and whites in their membership can do reasonably well as
long as the Blacks remain a numerical minority" (1979:60).
What happens in practice is that when Blacks become a majority the white members begin to fall off drastically. This
practice simply reinforces the reality of the homogeneous
unit principle. People prefer to believe in Christ and grow
in Christ without having to cross linguistic, class, or
racial barriers.

Some would argue that the Christian message has something to say to whites who abandon their Black brethren in this way. If racism and discrimination exist, surely this is wrong; however, if the issue is simply that Blacks prefer to worship and grow as Christians with Blacks, and whites prefer to worship and grow as Christians with whites, then the concern is not so much spiritual as it is cultural. Wagner cites an example from a well known evangelical church in Chicago:

> Even in a situation as unusual as Chicago's Circle Church where members of the white majority derive considerable satisfaction from their efforts to 'become blacker' through fellowship with black church members, the situation is fragile. Despite strenuous efforts to prevent a split; in fact, the blacks recently announced they preferred their 'funky Jesus' to the 'honky Christ' and started a new church designed to attract members from their own homogeneous unit. Blacks claimed that white members did not share a deep enough concern for justice. The difficulty of mixing homogeneous units on a fellowship level while still preserving adequate channels for communication and understanding among the members of each is hard to overstress (1979:61).

We must recognize that we live in a pluralistic world. This is true all over the world. Every country is composed of many ethnic and linguistic groups. Our own country is a prime example of dozens and dozens of ethnic groups with roots in Europe, Great Britain, Asia, Africa, and Latin America. Wagner strikes a sensitive note when he writes, "The new pluralism requires that people be accepted for who they are, recognizing that the group is an important component of their human identity" (1979:61). Because a group of people appreciate their ethnicity and enjoy growing together in Christ we must not consider this to be unethical or sub-Christian. It is only natural and their distinctive identity as a group needs to be preserved. As McGavran notes, "Christians must not betray and abandon their ethnic units in becoming Christian. They must not think of themselves as doing this, and they must not seem to others to have done this" (1979:14).

The Ethclass Model

C. Peter Wagner has developed a useful model as a tool to
discern with some measure of accuracy how American homogeneous units may be described in order to determine the social
framework within which churches can be expected to develop.
This model is built upon suggestions made by Milton Gordon
in his book, *Assimilation in American Life* (1964:51). According to Wagner, "Gordon's very helpful term 'ethclass' describes the subsociety created by the intersection of the vertical stratifications of society with the horizontal stratifications of social class" (1979:61).

Wagner has developed a circular model (see Figure 3) in
an attempt to depict significant components of a person's
group identity. The top half of the circle represents ethnic
considerations: race, religion, national origin, and assimilation factors. These are vital elements in the identity
of any group. Assimilation factors refer to how fast or how
slowly a group assimilates into the larger cultural majority.
The lower part of the circle depicts social class components:
economic status, vocation, formal schooling. These factors
affect personal interrelationships with other people, and
how well they are able to progress in social mobility. Also,
to complete the picture two other components are included:
regional identity and rural-urban orientation. It can make
a great difference whether a person comes from the Great Lakes
region or from southern New Mexico; from the greater Boston
area or from the cotton fields of Alabama. We all have a
tendency to associate with and appreciate our own kind of
people.

This model provides a useful tool for determing a homogeneous unit. Some of the factors are more difficult to
weigh, and some components will be more important than others.
This will be especially true with race, religion, and economic
factors. Nevertheless, using the ethclass model God's servants will find a tool which will enable them to understand
social structure more clearly. From that point on strategies
of evangelism and church growth may be developed. Wagner
feels that, "although there may be exceptions, to describe
an American ethclass is to describe an American homogeneous
unit" (1974:61).

Writing in *Church Growth Bulletin* (1980:18), Wagner refers to a synonym for the term "homogeneous unit." The term
is simply, "peoples." He states, "The Lausanne Committee for
World Evangelization, for example, has adopted the 'people

PRINCIPAL COMPONENTS
OF ETHCLASS IDENTITY--U.S.A.

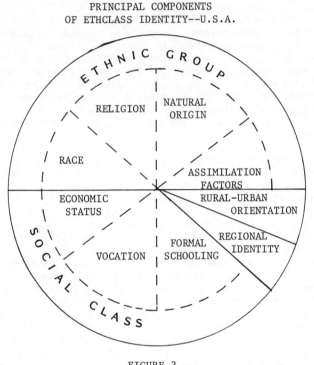

FIGURE 3
(Wagner 1979:63)

approach to world evangelization.'"   Instead of seeing the
world as composed of 221 countries it is more realistic to
perceive it consisting of about 25,000 people groups.   From
this number approximately 16,750 people groups do not yet
have a national church in their midst.   What is a people
group?   According to Edward R. Dayton in *That Everyone May
Hear*, a people group "is a significantly large sociological
grouping of individuals who perceive themselves to have a
common affinity for one another" (1980:25).

Factors which bind a people group together may be things like language, ethnicity, religion, occupation, residence, class or caste, situation, or various combinations of these. Some examples might be "Urdu-speaking Muslim farmers of the Punjab, Cantonese-speaking Chinese refugees from Vietnam in France, Welsh working class miners, or Tamil-speaking Indian workers on Malaysian rubber plantations" (Dayton 1980:27).

Ralph Winter, of the U.S. Center for World Mission, has suggested the term "hidden peoples" be used for the great number of people groups in which there is virtually no Christian group in existence. Such people groups are hidden from us and they need to be found. Writing in *Unreached Peoples '81*,[1] Wagner and Dayton of the Lausanne Committee for World Evangelization have noted further developments of the "hidden people" concept:

> The Strategy Working Group thus sought to absorb this valuable term as it further developed a hierarchy of unreached people: if there are virtually no Christians in a group, it is a hidden people. If there are as many as 1 percent, it is initially reached. Up to 10 percent, minimally reached. From 10 to 20 percent, probably reached (1981:26).

It is necessary to plan strategies for World Evangelization.[2] The people by people approach will be enunciated more clearly in the years ahead. The church has before it a great unfinished task. Identifying homogeneous units and planning strategies for their evangelization will challenge our best energies for years to come. Wagner sums it up well in these words:

> Modern anthropology has taught us that individuals group themselves together in social units more meaningful to them and to their neighbors than countries. The primary unit is the nuclear family, then the extended family,

---

[1] See also *Unreached Peoples '79* and *Unreached Peoples '80* (Elgin, Illinois: David C. Cook Publishing Co., 1979, 1980).

[2] Consult for further information the excellent volume by Edward R. Dayton and David A. Fraser, *Planning Strategies For World Evangelization*. (Grand Rapids: Wm. B. Eerdmans Publishing Company, 1980).

then the culture or sub-culture. These social
units are not accidental and externally-imposed
as are the boundaries of modern nation-states.
They are indigenous and consequently integral
to the personalities and the dignity of the
individuals that make them up. They constitute
the comfortable, taken-for-granted, social
environment in which human beings develop their
careers, select their mates, discover their
self-worth and formulate their worldview. They
are what we call homogeneous units. The missionary task remaining is best conceptualized
as reaching neither individuals nor countries
but rather homogeneous units (1980:18).

Some contemporary theologians and missions scholars are
not so enthusiastic about the homogeneous unit principle.
Some object to the acceptance of sociocultural insights
gained through anthropological and sociological disciplines
rather than from biblical and theological sources. Others
have expressed doubts and criticism that the homogeneous
unit principle is just another means to promote discrimination
and racism. They favor the heterogeneous approach and prefer
to emphasize that the conglomerate church of Jesus Christ is
one even though it contains members from several homogeneous
units. Hence, they advocate that a biblical local church
should include many different kinds of people ethnically,
socially, and economically.

While it is true that a true church should be wide open
to receive all who will believe in Jesus Christ, yet in practice most Christians prefer to worship and fellowship with
their own kind of people. A church should not turn away any
who wish to join its ranks. The "whosoever will may come"
concept should be employed, but at the same time people
should be free to choose, if options are available, where
they would like to affiliate for worship, fellowship, and
continued growth in Christ. Opportunities should be afforded
for various homogeneous unit churches to get together for
occasional worship services, the observance of the Lord's
Supper, and for informal fellowship. In this way the unity
of the body of Christ may be manifested and mutual respect
and appreciation may be fostered among Christians.

Soil Testing

The simple fact of varying receptivity of the Gospel
message must be recognized by every missionary. Often young,

zealous missionaries from the East have gone to the uttermost regions of the world with the idealistic notion that
people were just waiting by the thousands to accept the Savior.
Such a notion is far more fiction than fact. Now and again
there have been some very receptive populations, but this is
not the norm when it comes to receptivity. McGavran reminds
us realistically that, "the receptivity or responsiveness of
individuals waxes and wanes. No person is equally ready at
all times to follow 'the Way'" (1980:245).

Our Lord often spoke in agricultural terms about planting
seed, pruning, and harvesting. The work of proclaiming the
Gospel and church growth is much like that. There has always
been, from the very beginning, an unevenness in the growth of
the church. The Gospels tell us that the common people
listened to our Lord's message much better than the Phari-
sees and the Sadducees.

"Peoples and societies also vary in responsiveness.
Whole segments of mankind resist the Gospel for periods--often
very long periods--and then ripen to the Good News" (McGavran
1980:246). It was true in the first century when, for the
first three decades after our Lord's ascension, the Jews were
far more receptive than were Gentiles. Yet, later through
the missionary journeys of Paul and his team members, Gentiles
began to respond to the Gospel. Similar patterns of receptivity have occurred in more recent times. McGavran shares an
illustration from the Far East:

> Southern Baptists between 1950 and 1960
> maintained major missionary forces in Thailand
> and Hong Kong. In 1960 they had forty-two mis-
> sionaries in Thailand and thirty-eight in Hong
> Kong. The outcome in terms of people 'added to
> the Lord,' to use the Lukan phrase, varied enor-
> mously. At the close of the decade, in Thailand
> the membership of churches planted by Southern
> Baptists was 355; in Hong Kong it was 12,527
> (1980:247).

This case study of contrasting countries is most interesting and informative. First, the social structure of the
two peoples is quite different. The Thai are ardent Buddhists of the most conservative variety and have been somewhat
resistant to the Gospel for over 150 years; whereas, the
Chinese of Hong Kong have escaped from the Communist dominated mainland and have developed a new life style in a free
country which is a booming metropolis. Secondly, city peoples

are much more open to change., and Chinese are diligent and
willing to take risks much more than the ultra conservative
Thai. Thirdly, it seems obvious that the soil was ready for
planting and harvesting in Hong Kong, but in Thailand there
is yet need for much plowing, harrowing, and planting before
the harvest will be ready. However, here and there receptive
groups may be found who will respond to the Gospel gladly.
An example of this has been the Cambodian refugees who have
fled their homeland and are now residing in temporary camps
in East Thailand. Thousands of these Cambodians, having been
uprooted from their beloved country, have turned to Christ in
these camps. The political and social upheaval has created a
receptive people, and the Holy Spirit is doing that quiet work
of grace in many lives. Such conditions may not last for many
years; therefore, it is imperative for reapers to enter the
harvest while the field is ripe.

> The illusion which commonly claims churchmen
> is that they are working with one vast crop in an
> illimitable plain, all parts of which are equally
> favoured by sun and rain. The reality is that
> they are working with patches of land which tilt
> in every direction, are in various stages of dry-
> ness and wetness, and are covered with a huge
> variety of crops in every stage of development.
> Their task is not to labour everywhere, disre-
> garding the soil, crop, and degree of ripeness.
> Their task is to gather ripe sheaves into the
> granaries of God (McGavran 1966:42).

Not all areas consist of good soil ready to be planted
and harvested. A certain amount of soil testing is required
of God's servants. Missionaries must ask themselves hard
questions: What fields are ready for planting? Which groups
are likely to be more responsive? Where is there an un-
harvested crop which may rot in the field? Some areas will
need to be held lightly while other fields will require much
diligence in planting, watering, and reaping. "How populations are composed is a factor of great importance for church
growth. It is essential to discern each separate community
and its degree of readiness" (McGavran 1966:44).

Resistance-Receptivity Axis

It is helpful for missionaries to give prayerful consideration regarding the receptivity of any people group. Dr.
McGavran has suggested the use of a resistance-receptivity
axis. Very simply, this is drawing a line on a piece of

paper and designating one end "resistant" and the other end "receptive." Then, recognizing there are degrees of receptivity, the missionary should plot the various groups in his area on the line estimating their degree of resistance to or acceptance of the Gospel. Once this is done prayerfully, it will be obvious where the Holy Spirit is more likely to bless the Seed of the Word with a harvest. These areas may then be visited, worked, and prayed over, looking to the Lord of the harvest for the time of reaping. The various groups on the axis nearest to the "receptive" end may be considered winnable peoples. Every effort should be expended to bring them to a knowledge of Jesus Christ.

Some missionaries and mission administrators object to this methodology feeling that some areas will be overlooked purposely and the people will not hear the Gospel. To this objection Dr. McGavran replies:

> Recognition of variations in receptivity is resisted by some mission thinkers because they fear that, if they accept it, they will be forced to abandon resistant fields. Abandonment is not called for. Fields must be sown. Stony fields must be plowed before they are sown. No one should conclude that if receptivity is low, the Church should withdraw mission. Correct policy is to occupy fields of low receptivity lightly. They will turn receptive some day (1980:261-262).

There are many extrinsic factors which affect the receptivity of various peoples. Dr. McGavran discusses six common causes in his book, *Understanding Church Growth* (1980:248-256).

1. *New settlements*. People who have been uprooted by war, famine, economic dislocation or other calamity may be especially receptive to change. In their new settlement area they will need to make new friends and new adjustments to life. This is an excellent time to introduce the Gospel. They may well be receptive. A contemporary example of this would be the Cambodians in eastern Thailand. Many hundreds have turned to Christ, and countless others are open and interested.

2. *Returned travelers*. Travel has a way of changing peoples' perspectives. Soldiers who have served overseas have returned home with a new viewpoint. Such travelers may become most receptive to the Good News. The Church needs to be

alert for such peoples.

3. *Conquest affects responsiveness.* Following warfare when
a nation and its people have been defeated usually there is
a vacuum which results. Old values and allegiances have been
toppled, and so the climate may be ripe for presenting the
Christian message. In 1945 Japan was in this position following her defeat at the close of World War II, and there was
a great period of receptivity for about seven years.

4. *Nationalism.* Korea is an example of this phenomenon. Having been dominated by Japan from 1910-1950 there arose a strong
nationalistic spirit in Korea. The Gospel was being proclaimed and thousands turned to Christ. Following the Korean
War, 1950-53, when the North Koreans invaded the South there
was a tremendous period of receptivity to the Gospel and
church growth has been steady for the past twenty-five years.
This is a factor which the Holy Spirit can use in the growth
of the church.

It should be noted also that nationalism may become a
deterrent to faith in Christ.   Shintoism in Japan is a strong
nationalistic religion which binds the nation together and
produces a strong solidarity. Only a Japanese can be a Shintoist; hence, the threat of another religion such as Christianity seeking to win Japanese produces a nationalistic reaction. In order to be a loyal first class Japanese citizen
one must remain a Shintoist. This type of nationalism has
hindered rapid church growth in Japan. There is a Japanese
Christian church, but not like the fast-growing church in
Korea.

5. *Freedom from control.* Control may well hinder responsiveness to the Gospel. When controls are relaxed, people are
more free to listen and consider the Good News. Communist
countries of Eastern Europe keep a firm grip on their populations; hence, the spread of the Gospel is hindered. If in
the future these controls are lifted, it is possible that a
great responsiveness on the part of these now subjugated
peoples could occur. On the other hand, in times of persecution the Church has been known to grow and be purified.

6. *Acculturation.* "Acculturation is the dynamic process by
which a society in contact with other societies changes its
culture, adapts to the new situation, accepts some innovations,
and modifies its system" (McGavran 1980:256). Some groups
possess a stronger tendency toward culture change; consequently,
they readily accept new ideas. Such a tendency certainly

favors church growth as the Holy Spirit accomplishes His work of conviction and conversion.

Edward Pentecost in *Reaching the Unreached* (1974:91-109) suggests some additional factors which affect the receptivity of a people. Among them he notes dissatisfaction, culture change, economic change, linguistic change, religious change, and degree of Christian influence.

MISSIOLOGICAL IMPLICATIONS

The need to understand social structure is vital for the missionary involved in evangelism and church planting. Status and role considerations must be understood carefully. How the missionary is perceived by the nationals of the host society will greatly affect the way in which the Christian message will be accepted. It is very helpful for the missionary to know the ranking of people in the group he is trying to reach for Christ. Knowing who has prestige and influence may be useful in building evangelistic strategy. Winning low class people or marginals to Christ first will do nothing to encourage further evangelism among higher classes later. Basic knowledge of social structure is valuable in formulating strategies for evangelization.

An understanding of rural and urban peoples is helpful for evangelistic outreach. The sociocultural environment of people affects the way in which the Christian message is received. Winning people to Christ in the city will not be the same as in the rural areas. Cities must be reached with the Gospel. Jacques Ellul has expressed the opinion that God chooses the city because man has chosen it (1970:174). Hesselgrave believes the city is of special importance to missions for two compelling reasons: "First, God has always seen to it that His message was sent to the cities; second, cities are focal points of change" (1978:366). This tendency to change is a positive factor for evangelism in the cities. The church of Jesus Christ will need to analyze the city, identify its people groups, and develop strategies to evangelize the masses. The burgeoning cities of the world will be the stiffest challenge for missions in the years ahead.

An approach to rural peoples will be necessarily different. They are much more conservative and resist change. Nida has advocated four basic principles of approach to a face-to-face society:

1. Effective communication must be based upon
   personal friendship.
2. The initial approach should be to those who
   can effectively pass on communication within their family groupings.
3. Time must be allowed for the internal diffusion
   of new ideas.
4. The challenge for any change of belief or
   action must be addressed to the persons or
   groups socially capable of making such
   decisions (1960:110).

A growing understanding of kinship relationships will
help to facilitate evangelism and church growth. Unlike
North American society, many Asian, African and Latin American societies prefer to make important decisions as a group.
If a key individual in an extended family can be won to the
Lord, his influence and example may well affect other kinsmen in believing as well. The Holy Spirit often works
through family groups. Often clusters of families make a
united move to believe in Jesus Christ and to walk the Christian way. When they do, they find mutual support and encouragement within the extended family network. The family
as a whole exercises considerable control over its members.
McGavran has observed that,

> Persons do not exist as independent
> entities who make decisions entirely on their
> own, but as parts of a social whole. Their
> thoughts and feelings are conditioned and
> determined to a very large extent by the con-
> trol of the family (1980:255).

Thus, in many societies children are not free to believe in
Jesus Christ at the missionary's children's meetings. Decisions of such great import are made by the elders of the
leading families and they are discussed at great length.
Missionaries need to be aware of the kinship relationships
because they have an important bearing on evangelism and
church growth.

The Need for Adequate
Language Learning

One of the key areas in preparing missionaries for inter-cultural communication is the need for adequate language learning. Language is an integral aspect of culture. Since it is the vehicle of communication among people, it is expecially important for missionaries to know the language. In the course of their preparation for missionary service missionaries should recognize the importance of a positive approach, the importance of bonding with people, the weaknesses of the conventional language school approach, the strength of learning to speak by speaking, the importance of nonverbal communication, and the importance of fluency for adequate communication.

THE IMPORTANCE OF A POSITIVE APPROACH

Thinking positively about doing any task is a definite asset. It is especially true for language learning. Any negative thinking must be overcome by a positive approach in order to insure success.

You Can Do It!

Thinking positively about language learning is a crucial aspect of the learner's approach. Often language learners approach their task with fears of complex sounds, structure, and meanings. This is quite unnecessary. A positive attitude will be far more practical and beneficial. Thomas and Elizabeth Brewster advocate this approach:

>   You can successfully learn another language.
> Successful language learners--both children and
> adults--begin with an underlying knowledge that
> a language is learned rather than taught. And
> they know how to take advantage of the abundant
> resources available to them. These resources
> are the people who speak the language (1976:1).

Negative thinking is never helpful for language learning; it
becomes a great hindrance. The positive approach will be far
more encouraging, and who knows? Language learning may even
be fun! Why not enjoy it while you learn? A privilege we
refuse to be denied!

Other Have Done It!

    In many countries of the world today some people speak
two, three, and more languages. They make no big issue about
it. Rather, they accept it as a natural part of life because
they need to speak more than one language. One missionary I
knew, a Swiss co-worker, spoke Swiss German, German, French,
English, Thai, and Shan--six languages in all! Yet, in North
America many of us have grown up speaking only one language.
We are impoverished indeed! If one needs to learn another
language and earnestly wants to do it, then surely it can be
done. In this regard Larson and Smalley comment:

>   While previous experience and formal educa-
> tion are very important to every language learner,
> it is essential for him to realize that the world
> is running over with bilinguals who may have
> scarcely seen a pencil, much less used one for
> learning another language. Basically, if a per-
> son needs and sincerely wants to learn the
> language of a new community in which he lives,
> he will be able to do it, whether young or old,
> with or without a formal program of study
> (1972:20).

    Children in every country of the world learn their own
mother tongue plus other languages which are relevant to
their existence. If children are capable of learning languages, then surely a prospective missionary with God-given
motivation should be able to do so.

Common Excuses

    When it comes to the issue of learning a new language,
North Americans have been known to make excuses. Somehow the

thought of having to master another language seems overwhelming. Eugene Nida, who has been associated with missionaries over a period of many years, has noted four common excuses for not wanting to learn another language:

1. One of the most common is the complaint of being too old before taking up the task.
2. Some potential missionaries assume that because they are 'tone deaf' they cannot learn another language, especially a tonal one.
3. Some people assume that because they have never studied any foreign languages before going to the field, they are thereby handicapped for life.
4. One of the most common excuses for language inadequacy is lack of time (1950:3).

Each of these excuses could be overcome by taking a positive attitude toward language learning. While it is helpful to use the example of a child learning a new language as a model, there are also some drawbacks for those who approach language learning as adults. These are not impossibilities by any means, but are worth noting as one prepares for language acquisition. Nida suggests four reasons why we do not learn a language as well as a child does:

1. As adult missionaries, we have already acquired a set of language habits, and we have practiced them for fully twenty years.
2. We shelter our ego with all types of inhibitions and restraints.
3. It is also true that we do not have native parents who fondly try to teach us, who never seem to tire of repeating words, and who praise us for our feeble efforts.
4. We are not exposed to the taunting of other children who cruelly force conformity upon their playmates (1950:1-2).

Motivation is a Key

Motivation and need are both key factors for good language learning. Once genuine motivation is present, the capacity to master another language may be realized. Larson and Smalley state:

It is motivation that determines ultimate proficiency in a second language, motivation

usually fired by the recognition that one
language is not enough, motivation for at least
a token degree of dealienation, or if not dealienation, some more utilitarian purpose like a
better job, scholarly interest, or even the power
to exploit (1972:4).

Potential language learners are often concerned about aptitude. Linguists have studied the relationships between aptitude, motivation, and opportunity. In this regard Barney
and Larson have noted:

Three things affect getting a new language
well: (1) aptitude, (2) motivation, and (3) opportunity to learn. Aptitude is God-given; motivation
comes from within; the mission must arrange opportunities to learn. Aptitude is least important of
the three; motivation, most important. People
with very low aptitude can learn if they are moti-
vated. At the same time, people with very high
aptitude test scores may fail miserable at language learning, because they lack motivation
(1967:36).

A lesser known aspect of motivation has to do with the
will. It may sometimes be confused with enthusiasm. Thomas
and Elizabeth Brewster explain it this way:

Motivation to learn a language is an act of
the will. Some language learners make the mistake of equating motivation with enthusiasm . . .
but enthusiasm is an emotion. It ebbs and flows
in relation to how you feel, or how the world is
treating you . . . Motivation is a determination
which results in a decision of the will--'I will
learn.' The 'I will' is far more important in
language learning that the 'I.Q.' (1976:2).

Think Positively!

For many people negative thinking is the path of least
resistance. Instead they should think positively about language learning. As the Brewsters have discovered, many language learners start with a defeatist mentality. "They have
become convinced, usually from school experiences, that they
cannot learn another language. We are committed to encouraging learners, enabling them to successfully join their new
community and learn its language" (1980:209).

Many factors affect language learning. John Hickman draws attention to four variables:

> The quality of an individual's learning of a
> second language may be understood by looking at
> the following variables: (1) the general aptitude
> and intelligence of the individual; (2) the social
> and cultural context in which the two languages
> are learned; (3) the social and cultural context
> in which the two languages are used; (4) the
> attitudes held by the individual toward the second
> linguistic social group, and his motivation toward
> at least a partial identification with that group
> (Smalley 1978:643).

A positive approach is very important for effective language learning. Just to realize one can do it because thousands of others have done it is very helpful. Excuses must be put aside and motivation stimulated by positive thinking. Anyone can learn another language if he/she has a need to do so and earnestly desires to do it.

THE IMPORTANCE OF "BONDING" WITH PEOPLE

A vital aspect of identification with people is called bonding. Missionaries should recognize the need for bonding, what bonding is, and how to implement it.

The Need for Bonding

One of the best aids to good language learning is for the missionary to become intimately identified with the indigenous people whom he desires to win to Christ. Such rapport is vital to the process of language learning. Donald Larson has noted this need on the part of missionaries:

> Missionaries do not always join the commun-
> ities in which they reside and to which they
> seek to minister. Too often, the missionary
> lives at the margin of the community's center of
> activity, reducing his effectiveness considerably.
> Many such failures arise because the missionary is
> simply not ready to identify closely with his host
> community (1977:73).

It is true that missionaries often live in missionary compounds with other missionary families. They then make forays out from the compound into the indigenous community, but they

live apart and effectively isolate themselves from the people.
This procedure is not conducive to good language learning or
to good communication of the Gospel. There must be the willingness to identify with the people by living among them.

What is "Bonding"?

Studies on the relationships between human infants and
their mothers reveal the importance of bonding. The Brewsters
observed this relationship firsthand in the birth of their
first son by natural childbirth. The non-drugged newborn is
more alert during the first day than at any time during the
next week or two. It is during these first hours after birth
that an infant develops intimate close relationships with the
mother, called "bonding." It is very important for the child's
development psychologically and emotionally. The Brewsters
have noted an analogy between this bonding process and the
missionaries' identification in a new culture for language
learning.

> There are some important parallels between
> the infant's entrance into his new culture and
> an adult's entrance into a new foreign culture.
> In this situation the adult's senses, too, are
> bombarded by a multitude of new sensations, sights
> smells, and sounds--but he, too, is able to re-
> spond to these new experiences and even enjoy
> them. Just as the participants in the birth ex-
> perience, his adrenalin is up and his excitement
> level is at a peak. Upon arrival, he is in a
> state of unique readiness, both physiologically
> and emotionally to become a belonger in his new
> environment. But then . . . just as the infant is
> snatched away by the hospital establishment and
> put into the isolation of the nursery, so the newly
> arrived missionary is typically snatched away by
> the expatriate missionary continguency and, thus,
> isolated from his new target community. . .
> Bonding best occurs when the participants are
> uniquely ready for the experience. The way the
> new missionary spends his first couple of weeks in
> his new country is of critical importance, if he
> is to establish a sense of belonging with the local
> people (1980:4).

The benefits of this bonding process for language learning
are obvious. The new missionary will be hearing and using the
new language immediately after arrival in the new culture

when he is best prepared to enter into the host community as
a belonger. These early relationships with the people will
be most meaningful as language learning continues. The host
people will do all in their power to assist the new missionary with cultural adjustments and in speaking the new language. They will be most supportive at this crucial stage
of bonding. The prospects for continued language learning
will be excellent. In this regard the Brewsters comment:

> Gaining proficiency in the language is
> normal for the person who is deeply contexted
> and has his sense of belonging in the new
> community. But language study will often be a
> burden and frustration for the one who is bonded
> to other foreign missionaries. Normal language
> learning is essentially a social activity, not
> an academic one (1980:10).

How to Implement Bonding

One of the best ways to implement this bonding process is
for the new missionary to live for a period of months with a
national family. The attempt on the missionary's part to become an insider instead of an outsider as soon as possible is
a big step toward successful language learning. Living apart
in a mission compound has a tendency to produce negative reactions by the host community. Donald Larson comments on this
approach:

> Outsiders cannot live on the edge of a
> community without coming to the attention of
> insiders in a negative way. The term 'outsider'
> has negative connotations. So, the missionary
> must become an insider, at least to some extent,
> if he hopes to avoid these negative reactions
> to his presence and become a valuable person in
> the community (1978:158).

This approach requires a willingness for immediate cultural adjustment and identification with the people. It is
not without risks, but the dividends are great for the newcomer. The new missionary will be surrounded by natural
language helpers from the host family, and he/she will have
an excellent opportunity to learn both language and cultural
ways day by day. Of course, the missionary will pay room
and board to the host family during the period of living in
the national home. The opportunities for hearing the language
and for receiving correction in speaking are excellent. This

approach, although very demanding of the missionary at first, is well suited for genuine progress in language learning within the host culture.

THE WEAKNESSES OF THE CONVENTIONAL LANGUAGE SCHOOL APPROACH

Traditionally the language school approach to language learning has been employed by new missionaries. Certain weaknesses have been noted in the conventional language school approach. Let's consider some of these weaknesses.

Academic Instead of Social

The traditional approach of many language schools is more academic instead of social. Yet, language learning is a social activity and it must be learned through relationships with people. The idea seems to be carried over that because it is a school the activities within must be academic in nature. A husband and wife team, Thomas and Elizabeth Brewster, have visited many language schools all over the world. They have noted the strengths and weaknesses of these schools and their effectiveness in training language learners. Concerning the academic approach they have observed, "Another common problem is that language schools approach language and culture as bodies of knowledge to be memorized rather than as sets of skills to be acquired" (1976:128).

Language schools often spend much time on grammar rules, conjugations, and memorizing vocabulary lists. In some schools it has been noted that the teachers do most of the talking while the "language learners" have little opportunity to speak the language they are attempting to learn. Language learning consultants have been challenged to ask serious questions regarding the way many language schools approach the task of language learning. A more natural way may be the viable alternative. The Brewsters have seen a parallel between natural childbirth and language learning. Writing in *Missiology* (April 1980), they have called it "Language Learning Midwifery."

> The questions being raised are legitimate: Isn't there a better way? Is there any possibility that childbirth and language learning are natural processes which might work successfully without technological intervention? Can we choose to believe that God has endowed human beings with natural capabilities, and that they

therefore bring more than adequate potential
to these manageable, indeed exciting challenges? (1980:204).

Isolation from the Community

Another weakness of some language schools is isolating
the learners from the community of people who speak the
language. The discipline of a classroom schedule can be
valuable, but there is the danger that the learners will be
totally involved with the techniques and mechanics of language study and have little time in speaking the language
with the people in the community. Larson has noted that,

> No school can do the complete job. The
> principal value of a school is in teaching a
> person to learn how to learn: self education.
> Unfortunately, schools often over-insulate
> students and make them unnecessarily dependent
> upon teachers (1977:78-79).

It was this need that prompted Thomas and Elizabeth
Brewster to write a new book entitled, *Language Acquisition
Made Practical* (Lingua House 1976). This book develops a
step-by-step process to enable the language learner to know
how to study a language with or without the benefit of a formal language school. A daily learning cycle is set forth and
learners put it into practice immediately.

In their language learning classes the Brewsters assign
learners the task of finding an ethnic community nearby and
they must make friends there and locate a language helper.
Friendships are established and the learner begins immediately
to learn some of the new language day by day. There are four
parts to the daily learning cycle:

1. Prepare what you need for the day.
2. Practice what you prepare.
3. Communicate what you know.
4. Evaluate your needs and your progress, so
   you will know what to prepare for tomorrow
   (1976:10).

Classroom sessions are utilized to familiarize the learners
with the learning cycle, basic phonetics, and language learning helps. But, the real how of language learning takes place
in the community as the learner makes daily contact with his/
her helper and then practices the language with other members

of the host community. There is no isolation from people in
this approach; rather, there is intimate and daily contact and
involvement with people who know and speak the language.
Learners who have been through the LAMP program testify to the
effectiveness of this pragmatic approach in successful language learning.

Teaching Instead of Learning

The language school set-up easily becomes focused upon
the teachers and the mechanics of language. "It is interesting
to note that some schools even prohibit the students from talking with average people on the street" (Brewster & Brewster
1976:128). This is unfortunate because language learners must
have opportunities to practice what they have learned, and
they need the feedback from national speakers in order to
evaluate how they are doing.

In discussing their analogy of language learning and
natural childbirth, the Brewsters emphasize the natural--
people-oriented methods--of language learning from national
informants. They write:

> Women have been giving birth since Eve just
> as though they were uniquely designed for the
> process. Most women of the rest of the world
> find it a fulfilling and manageable challenge.
> Similarly, languages are learned spontaneously
> by virtually all children, and more than half
> of the world is multilingual. They learn lan-
> guage in the context of relationships and find
> their learning to be meaningful and manageable
> (1980:205).

When the learning takes place among people it is a rewarding
and challenging experience. At first it is demanding of the
missionary, but after a few weeks the sense of progress and
accomplishment usually motivates the learner to greater involvement. The traditional language school does not always
provide for this approach, and this may be seen as a weakness.

Compensating for Weaknesses

Not all language schools are weak in carrying out their
function. There are some good ones, to be sure. The missionary language learner will have to evaluate the school
where he/she is studying. If there are weaknesses discernible,
then he should compensate for these and thus improve the

language learning program. In this connection the Brewsters
state,

> Language schools almost never have all four
> parts of the learning cycle in their curriculum.
> Materials are prepared and practice is common,
> though often practice is insufficient to enable
> the student to use what he is exposed to. Sen-
> tence forms that may be more difficult (which
> you therefore need more practice on) are often
> saved to the very end of the course, when little
> practice remains. The most important step, com-
> municating daily what you know, is almost never
> part of the curriculum. Nor is self-evaluation.
> Curricular materials are seldom prepared with
> the immediate communication needs of the new
> learner in mind (1976:128).

If the language school set-up does not provide for conversation with nationals in the community, then the learner
should set aside time, perhaps in the early evening, to go
visiting in the community in order to practice the language.
It will be minimal involvement at first; that is, little to
say yet saying it with lots of people. But, it will grow and
people will encourage you to speak more and more of their
language. Larson and Smalley suggest,

> In general, a program should be so planned
> that the learner is able to use a large number of
> practical, concrete idiomatic expressions within
> a very few days. Then in a few weeks he should
> be able to express his needs in everyday matters.
> and to understand everyday conversations easily.
> Within three to six months he should be able to
> converse fluently, effectively and idiomatically
> with anyone he meets on a wide variety of every-
> day topics (1972:81).

The learner who has had an adequate background in language
learning will be able to supplement the language school program in order to make the most progress possible in the new
language. This will be challenging and beneficial for the
learner. The experience of understanding and being understood will be most encouraging.

THE STRENGTH OF LEARNING TO SPEAK BY SPEAKING

The saying that practice makes perfect might well be

stated, practice makes permanent. Practice is essential when learning any language--learning by doing and by mimicry. With practice sounds will become words and speaking will be a rewarding experience.

Learning by Doing

Learning by doing is a well-known teaching principle, and it certainly applies most appropriately to learning another language. Linguists and language teachers have established a necessary procedure for approaching the task of language learning. Nida states: "The scientifically valid procedure in language learning involves listening first, to be followed by speaking. Then comes reading and finally the writing of the language" (1950:21). Listening to national speakers is essential; then speaking the language should be the next step. The other two steps will follow along logically, but should not be employed before learning to speak the language.

The more a learner is able to listen and then begin to speak, the better his/her progress will be. Nida notes in this regard:

> Language learning means language using. A person never learns to play the piano simply by studying the mechanism of the instrument, observing the manual skill of others, and learning how to read music . . . to learn to speak, one must speak. One of the most common errors in language learning is the failure to practice hearing . . . He must get out where the language is spoken and where he can speak (1950:27).

This is excellent advice, and it works. Some language learners are hesitant to jump in and start using the language. They are afraid to make mistakes. One has to make mistakes in order to learn from those mistakes, and in the process the language will be learned. There is no point in delaying-- plunge in and swim like mad! Reading and grammar rules and books about language are no substitute for learning to speak by speaking. It works!

Importance of Mimicry

It is amazing that a skill as simple as mimicry can be so useful in language learning. Often teenagers, as they grow up, learn to mimic their parents or other family members.

If they are good at it they sometimes provoke the family no
end with their teasing. Nevertheless, this skill is vital
for language mastery. Nida declares that,

> Mimicry is the key to language learning.
> People who mimic easily have a great advantage
> in learning a foreign language, providing, of
> course, they will mimic native speakers. Mimi-
> cry consists of three phases: (1) acute and con-
> stant observation, (2) throwing oneself into it,
> and (3) continual practice (1950:23-24).

Acute observation is necessary in order to note how the
lips are rounded or unrounded, and whether the mouth is open
or mostly closed. Whether or not the teeth touch the lips
is important, and whether or not the tongue protrudes between
the teeth is likewise important for accurate mimicry. The
eyes and ears come into play for good mimicry. Of course,
some sounds in the new language are entirely new; thus, they
will need to be practiced with care. "A background in phonetics may be an especially significant experience for the
prospective language learner, for language study must always
begin with the retraining of one's hearing and production of
sounds" (Larson & Smalley 1972:20). Such training should be
vigorously stressed. Phonetics is a must for the prospective
missionary.

Mimicry has been utilized by millions around the world
when it becomes necessary to learn another language. Larson
and Smalley mention Singaporeans by way of illustration:

> A typical educated citizen of Singapore
> speaks Hokkien, Mandarin and English. If he
> was educated in Mandarin-medium schools his
> English is the weakest of these languages, and
> may not be functional. If he was educated in
> English-medium schools, his Mandarin may be the
> weakest of these. The strength of his Hokkien
> will often depend on whether it is used much in
> the home or not (1972:23).

Surely, if Singaporeans can learn two other languages besides
their own mother tongue, then North Americans should be able
to learn at least one other language well! Using mimicry
will be a good starter!

Speaking Brings Enrichment

Language learning is not all work. There is enjoyment in it. As the language learners progress in the language, they begin to be fascinated that nationals understand them when they speak. At times they may be tempted to think that no one will ever understand them. This is an over-anxious re-action and will lead to discouragement if allowed to persist. Language learning does take time, but it does bring a measure of enrichment as fluency develops.

> Until the new missionary can use the language
> to enrich himself, he can't take part in the every-
> day life of the community as an accepted member.
> Using the language symbolizes his membership and
> helps him carry out his work. Language study
> that gives the mechanics is fine, but if there is
> no chance for systematic enrichment, the new mis-
> sionary may not get the language as well as he
> should (Barnery & Larson 1967:35).

The more one speaks the new language and mixes with nationals engaging them in conversation, the faster one will master the ability to speak. Of course, everything will not be understood at first, but as time goes on much more will be grasped, along with the ability to respond appropriately in the national language. This is the strength of good language learning. The missionary must be a social creature and be willing to make contact with nationals. In the process the ability to speak will increase, and this achievement will bring a certain amount of satisfaction and personal en-richment. When the time comes to be able to communicate the Gospel in the new language, there will be an even greater sense of joy and achievement.

REALIZING THE IMPORTANCE OF NONVERBAL COMMUNICATION

Words, speech, dialogue and discourse are usually con-sidered to be the basics of communication. There is another dimension which must not be overlooked. Nonverbal aspects are vital for effective communication in all cultures.

What Is It?

God has created man with the capacity for speech; in fact, this capacity for speech is one of the chief character-istics which differentiate man from animals. But, all peoples communicate nonverbally as well. "In fact, it has

been reliably reported that in the average conversation between two persons (in our culture) less than 35 per cent of
the communication is verbal and more than 65 per cent is nonverbal" (Hesselgrave 1978:278).

When we use the term "nonverbal communication," what do
we mean?   "Nonverbal communication refers to the process
whereby a message is sent and received through any one or
more of man's sense channels, without the use of language.
Such messages can be intentional and conscious or uninten-
tional and unconscious" (Grunlan & Mayers 1979:100).

We use nonverbal indicators constantly without even realizing we are doing it. They become like second nature to us.
In North America we show irritation by frowns and biting the
lip. Boredom is revealed by a yawn or by deliberately fall-
ing asleep. Recognition and acceptance may be indicated by
a smile. Eye contact is important too. It shows respect
for the speaker and interest in what is being communicated.
Fellows may wink at girls to show an interest in them, or to
communicate a desire for further acquaintance. These are all
familiar nonverbal indicators to North Americans.

> The patterns of nonverbal behavior are
> culturally defined. Yes or no messages are
> conveyed by the nodding or shaking of one's
> head. These patterns are part of the arbitrary
> seletion of symbols of the culture. They must
> be learned, along with language and other aspects
> of the structure of society, by new members
> entering the culture (Grunlan & Mayers 1979:101).

People communicate far more than they realize via nonverbal indicators. Facial expressions, the nod of the head,
the use of the lips and tongue may all communicate messages
to others. What about such messages as that which is communicated by sticking out the tongue at someone--or even a kiss?
Both are nonverbal!

Body Language

Since the speech apparatus is not utilized in nonverbal
communication the body is used instead. This may be called
"body language" or kinesic communication. Peoples all over
the world have developed body language suitable to their
communication needs. In this regard Hiebert comments:

People have created media other than
language and writing to convey their messages.
Kinesics is communication by means of gestures
and body actions. Americans point to things
with their index fingers, a gesture considered
obscene in some societies, where the hand, head
or lower lip is used to point. Facial expressions convey a great many subtle messages in
ordinary conversation with the result that an
inexpressive or deadpan face is cause for unease
(1976:134).

In some cultures the interpretive dance communicates a
valued message to those who are insiders in that culture.
"In fact, in certain Southeast Asian nations the interpretive dance is the primary nonverbal means of communicating
to a group. The Thai easily read the symbolic message of
the formal dance without its being verbalized" (Grunlan &
Mayers 1979:102).

Touching behavior is a part of body language and it includes stroking, hitting, greetings, farewells, holding,
guiding another's movements. Hesselgrave adds, "It entails
such information as: Is group X a contact or a non-contact
group? How are greetings performed? With whom is touch
appropriate and in what situations (especially in contact between the sexes)?" (1978:283).

The more we think about it and analyze our behavior
patterns, the more we realize how much we are dependent on
silent language and body language for communication. Where
would many speakers be, especially some preachers, without
the use of their hands and gestures? Such gestures are a
part of body language.

Significance for Missions

In thinking of nonverbal communication and missions we
must realize that one form of communication in our culture
does not necessarily communicate the same message cross-
culturally. "For example, the occasional North American
hand wave of goodbye with the fingers pointed down is just
the opposite of the Latin American wave. The Latins extend
their fingers up for 'goodby,' and down for 'come here'"
(Mayers 1974:217). Thus, it may be seen that we may not
communicate exactly what we thought with our well learned
gestures.

In cross-cultural situations North Americans may cause frustration and consternation to others who do not understand our nonverbal communication. On occasion this may be offensive and cause temporary misunderstandings.

> Sometimes kinesic symbols cause much frustra-
> tion in cross-cultural encounters. North Ameri-
> can eye contact is far too intense for a Fili-
> pino, who tends to break eye contact early. He
> breaks eye contact (1) to show subordination to
> authority, (2) to differentiate roles, i.e., men
> and women or adult and child, and (3) to indicate
> that staring is not proper behavior. The North
> American, even though he places low value on
> staring, encourages eye contact to show he is
> respectable and trustworthy. A Filipino woman
> in a North American class, resisting the cul-
> turally determined eye contact of the professor
> cried out, 'You make me feel naked!' In other
> words, she was saying, 'You stare at me as if
> you want to see right through me!' (Grunlan &
> Mayers 1979:102).

It is quite apparent that the new missionary must try to learn nonverbal communication as well as verbal communication in the new culture. The missionary must be careful not to be ethnocentric in the realm of nonverbal communication. It is important that this mode of communication be learned and practiced so that it will become natural in the host culture. Its importance for missions is vital and not to be overlooked.

THE IMPORTANCE OF FLUENCY FOR ADEQUATE COMMUNICATION

The goal of the language learner is to become fluent in order to communicate with ease in the host society. At times this goal may seem to be elusive and unreachable. Yet, through hard work and adequate time spent, fluency is attainable, and the rewards are well worth the effort.

Fluency Means Work!

Every missionary would like to be successful in the missionary task. There are many variables when it comes to measuring success. Yet, one of the important aspects is gaining fluency in the language so as to be able to communicate effectively. Not all missionaries attain this goal. Donald Deer has studied the missionary language learning problem in Zaire, Africa, and reported:

What has gone wrong? I personally know of
missionaries who themselves traced their failure
to their inability to communicate, with all the
attendant frustrations. Others have probably
given up without being able to put a finger on
the problem, but in a very large number of cases
the failure to perform adequately in French and/
or an African language has obviously been a deci-
sive factor (1975:89).

In order to become fluent in another language there is no
substitute for working at it. Associations with national
speakers must be much and often. It is not the grammar books
and reading books that produce fluency, but constant associa-
tion and conversation with national speakers. Formal language learning situations are useful, to be sure, but the
informal social contacts are likewise most beneficial for
language learning.

It should be said, nevertheless, that if
missionaries had had more social contacts with
Africans in an informal setting, and done more
listening to Africans talking among themselves
. . . but social contacts have been woefully lacking. Most contacts between missionaries and
Zaireans have been in church, in meetings, in
the context of their work, and on the level of
employer to househelp--hardly the optimal context for language learning (Deer 1975:96).

Missionaries and nationals work together, but they do not
always play together. It is true that language study is work,
but times of play and social activities with nationals may
also be an enjoyable aspect of language learning. It is surprising how fluency will increase as the missionary takes
every opportunity to hear and speak the new language. Yet,
it is work, but so rewarding later!

Fluency Takes Time!

Not only is language learning hard work, but it is a time
consuming process. These two factors have a unique way of
combining to produce fluency in speaking the new language.
Effort and discipline are involved, and it must include intimate identification with the people. Languages are not
learned in isolation. Nida writes:

Linguistic training is of great help, but it is no substitute for cultural submersion. One Indian who had been trying very hard to teach a missionary the indigenous language explained with great distress, 'I do not know what to do. I have been teaching this missionary for a long time, but she just sits and studies, and seems to learn nothing. Why, a Spanish-speaking girl married one of the Indians in our village, and now in one year's time she talks very well. Why is the missionary ignorant?' The problem is not one of ignorance, but of cultural isolation, of learning a great deal about the language but not learning the language, of studying but not speaking (1954:223).

It takes time to be with people, but it is time well spent. Often missionaries are so concerned about the "work" that they do not allow sufficient time for adequate language learning. This is often true of doctors, nurses, and technical personnel who are usually in short supply. Consequently they are pressed into service too soon and without the benefit of proper time in language study. It can become frustrating. They usually regret it later. Nida has noted four reasons for failure in language learning:

1. Lack of time.
2. Some of the failure to learn a language results from the wrong approach.
3. Being taught the native language by some older missionary and without the constant presence of a native speaker can prove disastrous.
4. Another mistake in language learning is the habit of placing reading ahead of speaking (1957:8-10).

The time factor is one of the four reasons. Prospective missionaries must be trained and advised to plan wisely in order that sufficient time is allocated for language study. Fluency takes time--there is no doubt about it, but it is worth the extra time and effort.

Fluency is Worth it!

Becoming fluent in another language brings its own rewards. There is a peculiar joy and satisfaction about being able to share the riches of God's Word and the Gospel message among a people who have never heard it before or know little

about it.   Fluency at this juncture is a great asset to
effective ministry.   Sharing Christ with the people of another
culture and in their national language is the supreme purpose
of missionary endeavor.   The missionary should strive for
that goal and realize that fluency in the language is one of
the keys to achievement.

Becoming fluent in another language not only unlocks cultural ways, but may be a defense against outside opposition.
Nida shares a clear illustration:

> One missionary working in an Indian tribe
> Latin America was threatened by the local priest,
> and the natives were instructed to drive him out,
> but they defended their missionary friend by say-
> ing, 'We can't drive him away; he is one of us
> now.   He speaks our language.'   This missionary
> had gone out and lived with a native family, and
> in this way he had acquired an amazing facility
> in one of the most complicated Indian languages
> of this hemisphere.   His efforts were certainly
> not unrewarded in the response of the people to
> him and to his message (1950:12).

All the time and the hard work is worth it when the missionary witnesses dozens or hundreds turning to faith in
Christ and becoming responsible members of His church.   It is
then that fluency in the language takes its rightful place,
and the missionary is grateful for all that has transpired
in order to see the name of Christ glorified among those in
the "uttermost parts of the world."   Nida sums it up very
well when he comments: "Languages can and must be learned if
the Word of God is to be communicated in the words of men,
but this cannot be done outside of the total framework of the
culture of which the language in question is an integral
part" (1954:223).   Let's take the initiative in becoming
good language learners.   In this way God will enable us to
become better communicators for Him.

The Need for Adequate
Culture Learning

Basically there are two reactions to a new culture. "When people leave their own culture and move into a new culture, they can move in one of two directions—either toward empathy, acceptance, and identification, or towards culture shock and rejection" (Grunlan & Mayers 1974:25). It is necessary for missionaries to be prepared for culture learning. Adequate preparation for culture learning will help to minimize culture shock, and will aid in removing barriers to intercultural communication. Other aspects of culture learning will help the missionary to remove barriers in communication, to recognize and use the tools of relationship, to understand the importance of form and meaning, and to be able to relate cultural relativism and biblical absolutism in cross-cultural ministry.

PREPARING TO MINIMIZE "CULTURE SHOCK"

The missionary's adjustment to culture shock will determine how well or how poorly he will perform on the field. If one has been prepared from an anthropological perspective, it will help considerably in scaling the first high hurdle in his/her missionary career. Without this kind of help the adjustment may be more difficult and prolonged.

What is "Culture Shock"?

A person's reactions toward the new cultural environment

is called culture shock. This term refers to an individual's
reaction to cultural ways in a place where customs and behavior are quite different from anything he has known before.
Strange sights, sounds, and systems of doing things affect
different people in different ways. Louis Luzbetak, a Roman
Catholic priest and an anthropologist, recounts a rather
humorous example of culture shock which he experienced in the
highlands of New Guinea:

> I can never forget the mental jolt I received
> when I learned for the first time the measures
> taken by my cook to keep my bread fresh. He had
> observed how the wife of a neighboring government
> official used to wrap her bread in a cloth. My
> cook, Kaspanga by name, was a fast learner, so
> he decided to adopt the same practice. The jolt
> this time was like a lightning bolt: the cloth
> Kaspanga used was his own dirty 'laplap,' a cotton
> loincloth that had been worn by him during the
> daytime and by my loaf of bread at night. After
> this incident it was not hard for me to understand
> why an old, experienced missionary warned me upon
> arrival in New Guinea that the Commandment I would
> be tempted against most frequently would be the
> Fifth--'Thou shalt not kill'! (1970:86).

The new missionary is not yet accustomed to the strange new
ways; hence, there is a tendency to react with a measure of
shock and surprise.

We must not think that it is only missionaries going
abroad who experience culture shock. Business, embassy, and
military personnel also experience considerable culture shock.
For some who live in large cities amid a degree of affluence
the culture shock is only minimal. For others who live and
work among the common people in the rural areas culture shock
may be much greater.

Nationals from Asia, Africa, and other continents arriving in the United States experience culture shock as well.
Items which we take for granted, like flush toilets, television, microwave ovens, kissing in public, and Santa Claus,
strike the newcomers as very strange indeed--even shocking!
Some of the reactions may be positive and pleasing, but
others will be offensive and appalling. Cross-cultural contact provokes these kinds of reactions in all peoples.

Some people experience more culture shock than others do,

but gradually overcome it after a period of transition when
a person becomes more aware of the surroundings and the cultural ways of doing things. The missionary's hometown background has prepared him or her to function with a prescribed
set of cultural ways. When the missionary suddenly enters a
new cultural setting, it is only natural to expect that
things will be different. How a person reacts to that degree
of cultural difference is known as culture shock.

What Causes It?

When any individual enters a strange new culture, most of
the familiar cues are not to be found. Oberg describes it
this way:

> Culture shock is precipitated by the anxiety
> that results from losing all our familiar signs
> and symbols of social intercourse. These signs
> or cues include the thousand and one ways in
> which we orient ourselves to the situations of
> daily life: when to shake hands, and what to
> say when we meet people, when and how to give
> tips, how to give orders to servants, how to
> make purchases, when to accept and when to re-
> fuse invitations, when to take statements ser-
> iously and when not (1960:177).

Fear caused by anticipation of the new cultural experiences
can be a cause of culture shock. There is a sense in which
fear breeds fear. Larson and Smalley comment on this reaction: "Culture shock is sometimes aggravated by anxiety
resulting from the very knowledge that aliens overseas are
likely to suffer from it. It can produce its own vicious
cycle" (1972:39). There is no need for such fear if one is
prepared to expect culture shock and how to cope with it;
nevertheless, some people seem to prefer anxiety to careful
preparation for the task ahead.

One of the chief causes of culture shock may be identified in language shock. Language is a vital ingredient of
culture; hence, it must be considered carefully.

> Because language is the most important
> communication medium in any human society, it
> is the area where the largest number of the cues
> to interpersonal relationships lie. As the new-
> comer comes into a whole new world where he knows
> no language at all, he is stripped of his primary

means of interacting with other people, he is
subject to constant mistakes, he is placed on
the level of a child again (Smalley 1978:698).

During the early weeks in the new cultural setting the
missionary really feels the inability to communicate. All
his life he has communicated freely and with ease. Now the
situation is vastly different and the ability to communicate
easily is missing. This situation points to the need for
adequate language learning. It may be seen that language
learning and culture learning go together. There is no way
of separating them from real life situations.

Culture provides us with our general patterns for dealing
with problems. Smalley shares an illustration from his own
experience in Paris while learning French and living in a
boarding house with his wife and young son:

Even a loaf of bread could produce trauma.
At the first meal, when food was served, they
had no bread, although everyone else did. They
knew the word for bread, and asked for some.
This produced a bit of a flurry as the proprietor
cut a piece from the loaf on his table and brought
it over. This happened again at succeeding meals,
and the proprietor shared his bread with obviously
increasing reluctance.

The newcomers became increasingly uneasy, increasingly frustrated, concerned, as something was
obviously wrong. At this point the boarder whose
smattering of English was used for emergency purposes was able to convey to them the information
that everyone buys his own bread at the baker's.
It was not included in the price of board and
room. Reacting in terms of their own background
and expectations, and to the uncertainty they
had been feeling, the aliens were relieved to
know at last what the score was, but felt that
this was an utterly ridiculous way to run a boarding house (Larson & Smalley 1972:38).

It is easy to understand how this missionary couple experienced a measure of culture shock over something as simple
and common as bread. Also, the relief they felt when that
needed information was shared just at the time when they
needed it most. It is often the little things--the common
things of life--which cause culture shock.

How to Cope With It

As the missionary attempts to cope with culture shock three important aspects will need to be grasped: cultural awareness, involvement, and time. Working with these three aspects will enable the missionary not only to cope with culture shock, but to profit by it as well.

How vital it is for the new missionary to have a knowledge of basic cultural anthropology. Just to be aware of what culture is all about and what to expect will be ever so helpful. Larson and Smalley liken culture to a blueprint.

> Culture--as a blueprint--guides the behavior of people in a community and is incubated in family life. It governs our behavior in groups, makes us sensitive to matters of status, and helps us to know what others expect of us and what will happen if we do not live up to their expectations. Culture helps us to know how far we can go as individuals and what our responsibility is to the group (1972:39).

Being aware of cultural differences and having an attitude of acceptance of others will help immensely. The willingness to be adaptable, and the desire to adjust to the new cultural ways will help the new missionary in coping with culture shock.

Involvement as a learner in the new culture is another important aspect of learning to cope with culture shock. What can you do to get over culture shock as quickly as possible? Oberg replies: "The answer is to get to know the people of the host country" (1960:182). The new missionary will have to become a participant observer and get involved with people. The Brewsters heartily favor this approach.

> The missionary needs to be a learner before he can serve effectively. One of the essential things he needs to learn is the culture of the country so that he can make an effective contribution. Involvement in alien ways may be the most efficient device for building a bridge from one culture to another (Smalley 1978:887).

Since we learn by doing, it is wise for the new missionary to become involved immediately with the people of the host country. The missionary will learn to adapt by doing things

with nationals. They will be effective teachers of their
cultural ways if missionaries are willing to be good learners.
As the Brewsters comment,

> The general consensus is that cultural adap-
> tation cannot be taught but that it can be en-
> couraged and stimulated . . . One can learn about
> cultural empathy but it has to be practiced by
> trial and error before it comes naturally (Smalley
> 1978:887).

The third aspect of learning to cope with culture shock
is time. Time is on the side of the missionary and it is an
asset in overcoming culture shock. It is helpful over a
period of time to verbalize one's feelings with others who
are more culturally adjusted. Someone who has lived in the
culture over a period of years and has passed through culture shock will be a great help to newcomers. Oberg favors
this approach as he suggests, "Although talking does not remove pain, I think a great deal is gained by having the
source of pain explained, some of the steps toward a cure
indicated, and the assurance given that time, the great
healer, will soon set things right" (1960:182). Yes, time
will enable the missionary to grasp and use more of the language, and this achievement will help to unlock the cultural
ways of the people.

Time for making mistakes and learning from them will aid
cultural adjustment. Cultural awareness, involvement in the
host community, and time for understanding and adjustment
will combine to enable the missionary to cope with culture
shock. Certainly a good sense of humor--the ability to
laugh at oneself--will help to release tensions while the
adjustment process continues.

Cultural stress

Culture shock is usually of temporary duration while the
missionary adjusts to the new people and culture. "While
culture shock may pass rather quickly, culture stress may
hang on for months or years and mean the difference between
health and permanent or long-lasting injury" (Larson &
Smalley 1972:42). T. Wayne Dye, an erstwhile missionary with
Wycliffe Bible Translators in Papua New Guinea, suggests two
distinct kinds of stress involved in culture shock.

> One was the confusion and helplessness that
> arose from 'complete loss of cultural cues.' The

other was the stress which came from change to
a new way of living. I prefer to call the first
culture confusion and the second culture stress
(1974:62).

Dye has noted that some aspects of the host culture are
difficult for the missionary to accept and appreciate fully.
Hence, there is a measure of stress which results as one
lives among a people over a period of years. In studying
these factors, Dye has suggested a formula indicating the
ingredients which make up culture stress. New missionaries,
as part of their preparation for cultural adjustment, should
be thoroughly familiar with this formula. It will help them
in understanding what is happening before it actually happens:

Involvement	Value Difference	Frustration	Temperament Difference
————X	————————X	————————X	——————————X
Acceptance	Communication	Emotional Security	Inner Spiritual Resources

$$X \quad \frac{\text{Unknown}}{\text{Factors}} \quad = \quad \frac{\text{Amount of}}{\text{Cultural Stress}}$$

He explains it this way:

Increasing the value of a factor above the
line will increase the stress. Increasing a
factor below the line will reduce the stress.
No numerical values can be assigned; however,
the formula should not be interpreted in a true
mathematical sense. The relative importance of
these factors varies with the individual (1974:
62).

Here is another example of valuable insights which missionaries need as a part of their preparation for the field.
Culture shock is a reality within the context of cultural
adjustment. Yet, it need not be a formidable foe. Missionaries may learn what it is, what causes it, and how to
cope with it so that culture shock does not become an over-
bearing hindrance as they enter the host culture.

RECOGNIZING AND REMOVING BARRIERS TO
INTERCULTURAL COMMUNICATION

When a missionary first enters a new culture and meets

the particular people among whom he/she will work, it isn't long before the realization comes that barriers of communication stand in the way. Among these barriers three chief ones stand out: ignorance of the language and cultural ways, ethnocentrism, and time versus event orientation of the people.

Ignorance of the Language and Cultural Ways

The newcomer must enter the host society as a learner. At times he/she will feel most ignorant. As the newcomer begins to understand the language and cultural ways it will seem almost like passing through childhood again. Yet, this is a necessary phase of culture learning. Larson and Smalley help us to see the importance of culture learning:

> Culture gives us our general patterns for dealing with problems, some of which arise within the individual, while others come from his immediate environment; some of which come to us rather directly, while others come in symbolic form. Clothing and shelter, for example, are man's ways of coping with those problems which come to him from the physical environment. In eating and drinking he is responding to internal biochemical needs. Such psychological problems as loss of face, fear, and anxiety itself, involve symbolic behavior (1972:40).

At first the missionary is ignorant of these important aspects of culture, but as time passes that ignorance turns to knowledge and understanding. Thus, another barrier slowly topples over on the road to cultural understanding and adjustment.

Ethnocentrism

Mention was made of ethnocentrism and its dangers in chapter one. Ethnocentrism may be considered as a barrier to intercultural communication. Larson notes:

> The matter of ethnocentrism is pernicious-- not an easy one to handle . . . The missionary's ethnocentrism, manifested in narrowness and superiority, must be exposed and explained so that he can rebuild motivation for involvement with people of a different background (1977:80).

Unless the missionary has been made aware of ethnocentrism and its dangers, he/she may become extremely obnoxious to national Christians. Larson has alluded to the attitude of superiority which raises its ugly head when the missionaries function as if the way they do things is the only proper way they should be done. Our ethnocentricity not only affects our relationships with others--fellow workers and nationals--but also hinders language learning. As Nida has well stated:

> We should note briefly the fact that failure to learn foreign languages results primarily from false attitudes toward culture. A superiority complex fortified by a paternalistic air is about the worst liability for effective language learning. Our ethnocentrism makes it difficult for us to 'let ourselves go,' for we dread making mistakes, not realizing that languages cannot be mastered until we have thoroughly murdered them (1954:222).

Yes, ethnocentrism has a way of putting a barrier between ourselves and others. Thus, we make it more difficult for the Holy Spirit to do His work through us. So insidious is ethnocentrism that it may even affect our prayer life. Smalley recalls, "I heard ethnocentrism in a prayer recently, when a pastor thanked God that we were privileged to live in a culture so well suited to a Christian way of life" (1978: 712). Just being aware of ethnocentrism and its dangers will enable the missionary to be more sensitive to the needs of the people of the host country. Ethnocentrism need not remain a serious barrier. Missionaries should be willing to overcome it.

A missionary may learn to overcome ethnocentric tendencies. A willingness to accept others and to learn from them is a good starter. An attitude of humility will help nationals to see that the missionary needs to realize from the start that his way of doing things is not the only or proper way of doing them.[1] Recognizing and accepting the cultural ways of

---

[1]In reality most Westerners do not know how to relate to people of another culture. Also, they fail to understand their own cultural eccentricities. A very helpful book in this regard is James C. Stewart's *American Cultural Patterns: A Cross-Cultural Perspective*, (LaGrange, IL:Intercultural Network, Inc., 1971).

the people and allowing them to do things their own way will
definitely aid in overcoming ethnocentrism. Of course, some
cultural ways may be contrary to good health, prudence, or
biblical principles. In such instances the missionary will
need to use discretion. Luzbetak advocates empathy as a way
of overcoming ethnocentrism:

> Empathy means that the missioner fully under-
> stands and appreciates, as the local people do,
> the reasons behind their way of life. A mission-
> ary with true empathy views all native ways and
> values not through his colored glasses known as
> 'enculturation' but in full native context. With-
> out approving polygamy the missionary must under-
> stand why his people are polygamists, and without
> tolerating fetishism or promiscuity he must under-
> stand why his people venerate fetishes and are
> promiscuous. Empathy means that I understand why
> my people are what they are no matter what they
> are. Although empathy is internal, it is none-
> theless clearly perceptible to the local people,
> and it is a prerequisite for genuine apostolic
> identification (1970:96-97).

As the missionary learns to overcome ethnocentrism and begins
to practice acceptance, empathy and identification, the barriers to communication will come down. Instead the lines of
communication will be open to share the Good News of Jesus
Christ.

Time Versus Event Orientation

Missionaries from Europe and North America and other Western countries are notoriously time-oriented. We operate by
the clock. The nine-to-five mentality has become ingrained
into us, and it is natural to carry this orientation with us
overseas. However, we may find, as thousands of missionaries
have already learned, that nationals of Africa, Asia and Latin
America are far more event-oriented than they are time-oriented.
In many societies the people do not own wrist watches or
clocks at all. They operate by the sun, the moon, and the
seasons. Here is a potential area for tension and conflict
when the missionary wants to impose a strict time structure
to the activities of the church. Donald Banks comments from
the African perspective:

> This difference in orientation explains many
> causes of friction. Missionaries often complain

of 'African time,' implying the African is
unpunctual, and it is a constant source of
frustration why Africans are not punctual to
church services, arriving any time from the singing of the first hymn to the pronouncing of the
benediction. But for many Africans the event,
attending the service, is the most important
thing, and the time of arrival is relatively
trivial (1976:151).

It is true that tensions may easily arise when one society
is experience-oriented, whereas another society is time-oriented. Missionaries seem to enjoy pouring national believers
into time molds. Mayers has observed that, "The contrast is
striking when one enters the Philippines. The people are
more concerned with who is there and what is going on than
when something starts and ends" (1974:159). Americans sometimes have the tendency to emphasize being on time to such an
extreme that they destroy people by reprimanding them for
their tardiness or lack of concern for time. Such a practice
will hinder later communication.

It is entirely possible for a group of people to be time-
oriented in some cultural ways and event-oriented in other
ways. They are quite flexible and willing to bend in either
direction. It would be very helpful if missionaries could be
more flexible regarding time orientation.

These orientations pertaining to time are important for
missionaries to understand. A willingness to adapt to the
time frame of the host culture will be a positive step in the
right direction. The people may prefer a two- or three-hour
worship service with singing, testimonies, special musical
numbers, and several sermons instead of the traditional one
hour and one sermon service of the missionary. Let the meeting begin when everyone has arrived. Better still, let nationals plan and lead the meeting starting it when they are ready.
Unless respect is shown for the people's event-orientation,
effective communication of the Good News may be hindered.
Many tensions and frustrations may be reduced by eliminating
this barrier to intercultural communication.

RECOGNIZING AND USING TOOLS OF RELATIONSHIP

Culture learning will always involve relationships with
people. The missionary will have to learn how to relate
acceptably with people of the host country. Two very helpful
tools of relationship are cultural cues and functional equivalents.

Cultural Cues

Every culture has established ways of communication. People born into and raised in these societies are taught the appropriate cultural cues which aid interpersonal relationships. Mayers explains the origin of the term cultural cue and how it functions:

> The concept of cue is taken from the acting profession: the cue indicating the correct point at which the actor makes his appearance. Extended into the cross-cultural setting, the cue lets one do precisely what he wants to do, at the right time, and in the right way without manipulation. The cue may be verbal, as 'come in,' or it may be nonverbal, such as a wave of greeting. It may be simply the placement of furniture in a room. As a verbal cue it is tied into the larger linguistic pattern within the framework of culture, and as a nonverbal cue it is tied into the kinesics of body movements that are culturally established. As placement of object, it fits into that aspect of the culture termed, 'space relationships.' Society can be conceptualized as one vast, intricate network of cues (1974:216).

Each in his own society takes the cultural cues for granted. Here in the United States Americans shake hands when greeting someone. In Thailand if the uninitiated American extends his hand, the enculturated Thai will place his hands together, fingers extended and joined; then raising his hands toward his chin, he will bow the head slightly and say, "Sawaddi, Khrap!" This is the appropriate cultural cue in his society. Meanwhile the American is temporarily stunned holding out his right hand and not having it clasped by the new Thai friend. This is an example of a nonverbal cultural cue.

> Perhaps the largest number of cues to interpersonal relationships are the verbal ones. Stripped of the primary means of interaction, the language learner feels like a child again. . . . There at home he could handle himself; here he sounds like someone else; people laught at him; he feels rejected (Larson & Smalley 1972:43).

Verbal cues like, "O.K.," "Uh Huh!," "Phooey!," "Hi!," "Ummm!," and "Yeah!" are familiar verbal cues to most Americans, but international students coming to the United States to study find these idiomatic cultural cues a problem. They really have to work to learn them.

I recall a Chinese friend from Indonesia who came to the United States to do graduate study. His standard of English was good. On one occasion he was invited to speak at a church banquet. During the meal he was seated next to a fashionably dressed American lady who engaged him in conversation. Learning that he was from Indonesia she asked about local customs in his country. At one point he said something which stunned and surprised her. So, she retorted in typical American fashion, "Oh! You're pulling my leg!" Whereupon my Chinese friend was most upset and perplexed. Turning to the lady, in complete Eastern politeness and composure, he said, "Madam, I would never touch your leg!" Of course, we recoil with laughter at such a humorous situation, but for my Chinese friend it was not funny at the time. It was simply a misunderstood cultural cue. When I explained it to him afterwards, he smiled and understood immediately what the lady was trying to say. Many such stories could be told to illustrate verbal cues.

When the missionary goes abroad to another society he must try to learn as many cultural cues as possible--both verbal and nonverbal.

A knowledge of the cultural cue is needed by the agent of change so that he can adapt to the new society without losing his identity as a person and as a member of his own society. In other words, he must know the cue to remain a man of principle and to fulfill responsibly his role in life (Mayers 1974:217).

Functional Equivalents

Most people expect to find in another culture similar patterns of behavior to the ones they know in their own culture. Thus, when they go abroad as missionaries they are surprised to find things quite different from what they had anticipated. It is here that an understanding of the term "functional equivalent" is useful. The functional equivalent is rooted in meaning out of which form emerges and develops. It is the function and meaning which is important and must be communicated.

A functional equivalent is the form of one social and linguistic system that expresses the

meaning intended by a different form in a distinct
social and linguistic system. It is to be differ-
entiated from the direct equivalent which seeks to
maintain the same form across cultural boundaries
(Mayers 1974:11).

The form may well change with the passing of time resulting from technological developments. When the first automo-
bile was produced it was called the "horseless carriage" because the chief means of conveyance at that time was the
horse and buggy. Thus, we may say the contemporary automo-
bile is the functional equivalent of the horse and buggy of
a bygone era. The function remains the same--a means of con-
veyance--but the form has radically changed.

Other illustrations may be helpful at this point. In the
line of foods, rice is the functional equivalent of potatoes
in Southeast Asia and the Far East. They grow potatoes in
these areas, but they are definitely not the staple food
which is consumed. Also, chopsticks are the functional equivalent of the fork in China, Taiwan, and Japan. Most Americans
eat with chopsticks only with great difficulty and much impa-
tience. A person from the Far East eats with ease using the
"cutlery" of the East. In contemporary China the two-wheeled
bicycle is the functional equivalent of the American family
car. The average person in China does not own or use a car.
Most people ride a bicycle.

When it comes to the realm of language in crosscultural
communication there are some concepts and words for which
functional equivalents are difficult to find. Yet, in order
to communicate meaning well a functional equivalent must be
employed. In the King James Bible rendering of the letter to
Philemon the word "bowels" is found three times (see Philemon
verses 7, 12 and 20). During the early 1600's this term meant
something quite different from what it does today. So, in
contemporary English translations the word "heart" is used as
a functional equivalent. The meaning in the passage is the
same but the form has changed during the intervening years.
Over a period of years words do change their meanings. "No
functional equivalent can be expected to equate across cultural boundaries one hundred per cent. Thus, functional
equivalents may involve a range of equivalent items that do
in one culture what one of them alone does in another (Mayers
1974:219).

This is all a part of culture learning. Cultural cues
and functional equivalents are both important aspects of

learning how to communicate in another society. These are
tools of relationship which may be employed in order to be
a participant in a different cultural system. Given time
and experience these tools will greatly aid the missionary
during the process of culture learning.

RECOGNIZING THE IMPORTANCE OF FORM AND MEANING

All cultures are made up of structural units. These
structural units consist of some basic meaning or significance and a way of expressing that significance. The building blocks consist of forms functioning in certain ways with
specific meanings intended.

What is the Form/Meaning Composite?

The combination of meaning and expression of meaning
could be called the form/meaning composite. Mayers explains
it this way:

> Form/meaning composite of f/m, is the
> correlation of meaning with its expression,
> the form of expression communicating the
> specific meaning intended. In the process
> of change the form may remain constant while
> the meaning changes or is lost completely as
> in the case of survivals. In certain cases,
> the meaning will remain constant and the form
> will change and become more varied, producing
> a number of expressions communicating the same
> meaning (1974:10).

All cultures are constantly changing. New meanings become
attached to existing behavioral forms or old meanings may be
forgotten.

> An illustration of this is the lapel button-
> holes on men's business suits, which once served
> the useful function of buttoning up the collar.
> Nowadays, they are almost meaningless and are
> often omitted altogether. The result of such
> changes is often 'cultural lag,' in which forms
> and meanings change out of phase with one an-
> other (Hiebert 1976:29).

In carrying out the missionary task God's servants have the
responsibility to communicate a message that will be understood. This task is easier said than done. Form and meaning

become important structural units in this process. There must be a correlation between the two or distortion and failure of communication results.

Nida suggests that it is not enough to know the form of a cultural feature or even its value. It is necessary to know its function. He alludes to the form of a wedding ring in our culture. It has deep sentimental meaning to the one who wears it.

> But what is its actual function, apart from serving as a part of the wedding ceremony? For one thing, it marks married persons (Private Property, No Trespassing!), and as such it tends to promote the stability of marriage (1954:44).

This is a clear illustration of both form and meaning in a context all North Americans will readily understand.

In Africa a different form operates; namely, the payment of cattle as a kind of bride price. In reality it is more an equilibrium of compensation payment, for it compensates a clan for the loss of a member. Nida states that the bride price "has a meaning of legalizing the marriage and legitimatizing the offspring. The function of such a bride price is very similar to the ring in our culture for it also increases the stability of marriage" (1954:44).

In our contemporary North American society many ladies, and even some men, wear a cross as a necklace. If they were to be asked what the meaning of that is to them personally, many would confess that it has little or no meaning. It is just a piece of aesthetic jewelry to wear; hence, an expression of beauty. For some the cross might be worn as a good luck charm. In such cases there is a form which is utilized, but it lacks the original meaning for which the cross was intended.

Restructuring a meaning occurs in crosscultural contexts. Nida comments in this regard,

> When a communication takes place between sources and receptors who have different cultural backgrounds, one must expect a high degree of restructuring of meaning. That is to say, whatever concepts are communicated are reinterpreted in terms of the total conceptual framework of the different context (1960:87).

An illustration of this may be found in considering the post
World War II situation in Japan. Following the war American
evangelists preached to hundreds of thousands of people. At
the close of the Gospel presentations, as they would normally
do in the United States, the evangelists gave an invitation
for the Japanese people to accept Jesus Christ as Savior. If
they wished to make this decision, they were asked to raise
their hands. Of course, thousands did so, and reports were
wired back to the United States saying many thousands had
turned to Christ for salvation.

Missionaries who knew Japan and Japanese culture well
explained that those who responded by raising their hands,
for the most part, were simply doing what they felt the   ‹-
speaker wished them to do. Not to respond accordingly would
be impolite for a Japanese. Here the form of hand raising
was correlated with the meaning which Americans understood
from their cultural background. Such situations produce
gross misunderstandings and often much confusion on the part₂
of the receptors.

Language has Form and Meaning

Language may be perceived as two distinct symbolic systems: the verbal and the written. Sounds in a language are
arbitrary. This may be illustrated in the use of the English
vowel "a." "An English 'a' can represent any number of different pronunciations phonetically, such as 'father,' 'rat,'
'share,' 'amount,' etc." (Mayers 1974:197). These are, in
fact, different sounds even though we use the same written
symbol for all of these words. Only those who are enculturated are able to pronounce these words correctly according to
the American pronunciation. Britishers would pronounce them
differently, following the pattern learned in their country.
The word "grass" would be pronounced differently by an American and a person from Great Britain.

Language is passed on from generation to generation.
Everyone entering a society by birth or by migration is expected to learn the symbolic system for speaking. "All of
language grows out of the lived experience and represents
some aspect of that lived experience. The spoken language
is the basic symbolic system that is then taken and formally
symbolized by the writing technique or orthography" (Mayers
1974:197).

Any language, as a symbolic system, is quite adequate for
the handling of all the needs of the society. Missionaries

must learn the language of the people among whom they live and serve. The forms and meanings within each language are important for adequate communication. Thus, the form/meaning composite is a consideration which missionaries must not over-look. It will take time to master, but it is most essential for culture learning.

Culture has Form and Meaning

A group's total life-way is symbolized in much the same way as language is. Culture may be perceived as a symbolic system. Mayers illustrates it this way:

> The flag of a nation stands for its integrity and identity. Heroes are representative of the highest values of a society. A stop sign is a symbol of traffic control, as are yellow lines in the middle of the street. Uniforms are symbolic of a person's status or standing or role within a society (1974:197-198).

It is helpful for the missionary to recognize that unless meaning and form are present there is no symbolic reference. Should a form exist without the meaning the form is sterile and is commonly referred to as a "survival." Most cultures seem to have examples of survivals which exist in the present but often their meanings are lost in the past. For instance, why do men's business suit jackets have buttons sewed onto the sleeves? They serve no present function today, but per--haps in the past they did serve a useful function. Today they seem to be a survival of the past.

Form and meaning are significant aspects of both language and culture. As symbolic systems they must be learned and understood in order for a person to function as a respon-sible member of that society. Missionaries must of neces-sity be careful to consider the form/meaning composite as they involve themselves in culture learning.

SUMMARY

Surely it is obvious that the need for adequate culture learning is an important one for the missionary. Discourage-ments and frustrations may be minimized if missionaries are better prepared in this vital area. There is a sense in which God's servants are constantly learning about and try-ing to understand the culture and people where they live and work. It is truly an ongoing process.

Preparing for culture shock by understanding what it is and how to cope with it will be an asset. As missionaries learn to remove barriers to intercultural communication, they will find new and greater openness in sharing the Good News. Working with the tools of relationship—cultural cues and functional equivalents—will also help in the culture learning process. An understanding of the importance of form and meaning will open up areas of communication by focusing upon the significance of symbolism and how difficult it sometimes is to communicate clearly across cultural barriers. The missionary who is aware and prepared in these areas will be in a stronger position to participate more effectively in intercultural communication.

The Need to Understand
the Importance of Worldview

A missionary needs to understand the basic worldview of
the people to whom he goes with the Good News. In simple
terms, worldview refers to how people understand the world
around them. Is it friendly or unfriendly? Is it filled
with spirits, or is it scientifically and rationally explain-
able? How about its origins and functions? What causes
sickness? These areas all relate to worldview.

It is not always easy to obtain accurate worldview information, but it is most useful when available. At present
worldview studies are in a fluid state. As Kearney suggests,
"Worldview is not a well-established field of study in the
sense that it appears in course catalogs, or that there are
recognized schools of worldview theory or many scholars
specializing in it" (1975:247). Helpful insights pertaining
to a specific people and their culture may be gained from
careful research regarding worldview considerations.

RECOGNIZING THE IMPORTANCE OF WORLDVIEW

The missionary finds, as he studies the worldview of a
people, that these considerations affect every aspect of their
life-ways. It is rewarding to seek answers to questions like,
what is worldview? Why is worldview important? And, how
does worldview affect communication?

What is Worldview?

As the term implies, worldview basically refers to the way

in which a group of people view the world around them. It
has to do with basic assumptions and understandings of the
world and man's relationship to it. In describing worldview Robert Redfield offers some helpful criteria:

> Worldview may be used to include the forms of
> thought and the most comprehensive attitudes to-
> ward life. A worldview can hardly be concerned
> without some dimension in time, some idea of past
> and of future; and the phrase is large enough and
> loose enough to evoke also the emotional 'set' of
> a people, their disposition to be active or con-
> templative, or resigned, to feel themselves dis-
> tinct from what is 'out there.' or to identify
> themselves closely with the rest of the cosmos.
> It is the structure of things as man is aware of
> them. It is in the way we see ourselves in rela-
> tion to all else (1958:86).

Redfield's criteria enable us to get a handle on the breadth
of understanding which worldview covers. There is a sense
in which a group's worldview organizes their understanding
of life and the world all around them. Marguerite Kraft
noted that, "Goodenough (1957) viewed culture as not consisting of things, people, behavior, or emotions, but as the
forms or organizations of these in the minds of people" (1978:
6). It is noteworthy here that although Goodenough refers
to culture he is really talking about worldview when he men-
tions forms or organization which exist in the minds of the
people.

Worldview considerations cover a broad area. For our
purposes, let us consider that the worldview of a people
reflects their basic assumptions, values, and understandings
regarding life and the world in which they live. Worldview
considerations pertain to the areas of time, space, causation
(origins), the supernatural, and interpersonal relationships.
A few illustrations may be helpful at this point.

Some animistic groups hold the view that the earth is
ruled by spirits. Some spirits are good and some are evil.
At planting time, for instance, before the ground is broken
for planting, a carefully prescribed ritual takes place to
appease the spirit of the ground and to insure that a good
crop may result.

Some animists believe rivers have a spirit. Among the
Northern Thai people of Thailand, even though they are nomi-
nally Buddhist, there is the strong animistic belief that

before a stream may be dammed up for irrigation purposes the spirit of the stream must first be appeased. I recall on one occasion going with a group of Northern Thai men to dam a stream. When we reached the selected location for the dam I noted a simple bamboo altar had been erected near the river bank. On the altar a pig's head was placed. When I asked the foreman of the work crew for an explanation of this phe- nomenon, he told me the pig had been slain as a sacrifice to appease the spirit of the stream. This act was necessary prior to the construction of the bamboo-stake, rocks and mud dam. Where did this worldview come from? It has been passed down from generation to generation by the people because this is their perception of the world around them.

Disease theory is based upon worldview as well. Some animistic groups believe that when a person becomes ill an evil spirit has entered the body. This spirit must be driven out; hence, the shaman functions in their system as the cul- turally acceptable practitioner to drive out evil spirits in order that sick persons might recover. Their worldview per- ception leads them to these conclusions, and their practices over centuries of time bear out the reality of this theory in actual life situations. Such considerations will enable us to expect that worldview is something of major importance in understanding another group of people.

Why is Worldview Important?

It is important for the missionary as an outsider to be- come an insider as soon as possible. This always takes time and it presupposes a good mastery of the language, but it is a goal toward which the missionary should be moving. Margue- rite Kraft highlights the importance of becoming an insider:

> The outsider cannot see ideas, presuppositions and values. Insiders often cannot verbalize the worldview because it is not necessarily explicit in their own minds. Since worldview is largely acquired unconsciously, the insider takes it for granted and often does not question it or examine it. But language reflects and reveals a people's concepts and values (1978:5).

Once the missionary becomes an insider, even though at first it will be in a limited way, he will begin to identify with people. Gradually his understanding of what makes them tick will become more apparent. More and more it will be seen that this worldview encompasses the people's total response to their universe. Hiebert comments:

> Behind the observable patterns of human
> cultures seem to be certain assumptions about
> the way the world is put together. Some of these
> assumptions, called existential postulates, deal
> with the nature of reality, the organization of
> the universe, and the ends and purpose of human
> life. Others, values and norms, differentiate
> between good and evil, right and wrong. Some of
> these assumptions are made explicit in the be-
> liefs and myths of the people. Others appear
> to the anthropologist to be implicit in people's
> behavior. Taken together, the assumptions the
> anthropologist uses to explain a people's total
> response to their universe are sometimes called
> 'worldview' (1976:356).

Each of the areas mentioned above are significant in
helping the missionary to identify with the people and to be
able to understand their ways. To overlook the importance
of these considerations would only serve to jeopardize future
ministry among the people. The whole area of worldview is
relevant for the missionary in his work. Every effort should
be made to research and comprehend the worldview of the receptor people.

How Does Worldview Affect Communication?

There are at least three ways an understanding of worldview affects communication. First, a good grasp of the language will greatly help in acquiring an understanding of
worldview. Such an approach will also help the missionary
to become an insider and be able to identify with the people.
The relationship between language and worldview are closely
intertwined. Knowing the former well will unlock a greater
understanding of the latter. Larson states:

> Learning another language and becoming
> part of another community also involves one's
> assumptions, beliefs, and values. It involves
> his accumulated knowledge and experience, es-
> pecially that which brings views of man, lan-
> guage, culture, theology and mission together.
> These core presuppositions are the locus of
> the problem. They shape and influence the
> missionary's motivations and desires to become
> part of another community and learn its language
> (1977:75).

As more and more of the worldview is revealed and understood, the language and culture learning will be enhanced. As a result, the missionary will be in a better position to communicate in the language and thought forms of the people. Such a goal is worth achieving.

Secondly, worldview will provide a basis for hearer-oriented communication. It is perfectly natural for the missionary to minister from a speaker-oriented viewpoint. A better understanding of the worldview of the people will modify this perspective. One-way communication should be avoided and then the message has a greater potential to be understood. Marguerite Kraft is strongly convinced of this as she writes, "It is my premise that a people's concepts, basic presuppositions, and experiences affect the way the message of Christianity is heard and interpreted. Understanding the worldview is a necessary basis for effective hearer-oriented communication" (1978:4). Every missionary should be concerned to communicate the Good News in this manner. Such has not always been the case in missionary experience. Hesselgrave shares the opinion.

> One reason why much missionary communication has been monological (one way--missionary to respondent) is that missionaries have not been conversant enough with worldviews other than their own. In ignorance of what is happening in the decoding process, they have simply 'related' (!) the gospel. One gets the distinct impression that in some cases the motivation is to deliver the soul of the missionary rather than to save the souls of those who hear him (1978: 130).

Thirdly, understanding worldview will aid communication by revealing the culture's systems and the basic nature of the universe. As Hiebert explains,

> Each person organizes his day-to-day interactions with his natural environment by means of technological systems, and his relationships with his fellows by means of social systems. Via religious systems, he explains the fundamental nature of the universe and his own place in it. Religion, in other words, is the model man uses to explain the reality of all things (1976:356).

Knowing these systems and how they operate will enable the

missionary to unlock the secrets of the culture and how it functions. With this knowledge in hand communication will be strengthened as the Christian message is shared among the people.

Understanding the what, the why, and the how of worldview and its importance in understanding people will aid the missionary in becoming an effective communicator for Jesus Christ in another cultural setting.

WAYS OF PERCEIVING THE WORLD AROUND US

As anthropologists have studied people around the world, they have learned much about how different peoples perceive the world around them. Not all peoples see things in the same way. As Hesselgrave notes,

> The way people see reality can be termed their worldview . . . A worldview is the way people see or perceive this world, the way they 'know' it to be. What men see is in part what is there. It is partly why we are. But these combine to form one reality (1978:125).

As people look at the world around them they share varying perceptions regarding time, space, and causation. These perceptions color their life-style throughout their existence.

Time Perception

Some groups of people perceive of time in one way, while still other groups perceive of time in an altogether different perspective. Keesing elaborates on this aspect:

> Florence Kluckhohn suggested that the dominant value profile of a culture can be effectively explored in terms of a number of trichotomies (three-dimensional categories). The view of life of a people may, for example, be oriented primarily toward the past, the present, or the future; toward looking on the universe as basically evil, as neither good nor evil (mixed), or as good; toward seeing man as subjugated to nature, in nature or over nature. In the first category, for example, traditional Chinese values are strongly oriented toward the past, Hispanic values toward the present, and American values toward the future (1971:394).

These basic, undergirding time structures will affect behavior
and life-styles within a particular society. Not only are
traditional Chinese values strongly oriented in the past, but
also many African groups have a similar orientation. By way
of illustration, both Chinese and Africans have a profound
respect for ancestors who have passed on. The question has
been raised by missionaries in China and Africa concerning
ancestor worship. Is there actual worship of ancestors involved, or is it merely great homage and respect for these
dear loved ones? This becomes a missiological problem; hence,
a clear understanding of time perception as it relates to
worldview would be extremely useful for the missionary.

     As we have already seen, another aspect of this time
structure pertains to whether a given people are time-oriented
or event-oriented. North Americans and Europeans tend to be
strongly time-oriented, whereas Asians, Africans, and Latin
Americans tend to be much more event-oriented. The way work
is accomplished and the way personal relationships function
will be affected by this basic time perception. The missionary must learn how the people perceive of time. It may well
be quite different from the missionary's perspective.

Space Perception

     A group's geographical setting will affect the way in
which space is perceived. A child brought up on the broad,
flat plains of Kansas or Saskatchewan will perceive of space
quite differently than a Black brought up in the ghetto of
New York City. To the first, the great, wide-open spaces
will be the norm, but to the second, a dark, dingy, cramped
apartment on the sixth floor of a huge building sandwiched in
between two other buildings of nearly the same size will be
the norm. Both will experience life, but they will perceive
it differently.

     An ancient belief of the peoples of Thailand suggested
that the structure of government was determined by the belief that mankind was constantly influenced by forces emanat-
ing from the direction of the compass and from the stars and
planets--forces which could produce welfare and prosperity or
work havoc. As Blanchard explains it, "Harmony between the
empire and the universe was achieved by organizing the empire
as a small-scale image of the universe" (1958:91). Eliade
expands on this perception by adding,

          Siam was divided into four provinces with
     the metropolis in the middle; and in the center

of the town stood the royal palace. The country
was thus an image of the universe, for according
to the Siamese cosmology, the universe is a quad-
rangle with Mount Meru in the middle. Bangkok
is called 'the celestial royal city, the city of
the gods' (1976:24).

Thus, it may be seen that the Thai perception of the universe
affects the earthly layout of a major city. To them space
relationships which are linked to their worldview are very
important.

The behavior of people in interpersonal relationships is
likewise affected by space perception. It is amusing to contrast American ways with Latin American ways regarding the
distance between two persons during a conversation. Noting
Silent Language, by E. T. Hall (1959), Hiebert reflects,

Americans discussing general social matters
stand about four or five feet apart, often at
right angles to each other. It is important to
avoid the smell of the other's breath; however,
if they are discussing personal matters, they
move closer to each other and drop their voices.
Intimate communication takes place within the
two foot zone (1976:35).

Latin Americans enjoy a much closer person-to-person relationship in conversations. When a Latin talks with an
American he steps closer, and at the same time the American
takes a step backwards. This reaction will cause the Latin
to move closer again to continue the conversation; however,
the American will take another step backwards. Unless fore-
warned, neither may be aware of the conflict in the use of
space, and each may be thinking that something is wrong. The
reactions are simply caused by different perceptions of space
relationships. Each group may perceive of such space relationships in a slightly different manner.

Causation Perceptions

Two key areas of causation which most peoples attempt to
explain are the origin of the earth, and what causes disease
and death. Non-literate peoples may have the perception
that many years ago their ancestors came out of a hole in the
ground. This is a part of their worldview and it is passed
on from generation to generation. All members of their group
will hold this view. Other groups will hold differing views

of causation which are satisfying to them.

The cause of disease and death are challenges to all peoples everywhere. When people from different cultures disagree on the explanation of disease and death, how can they understand each other? Animists believe that sickness and disease are caused by an evil spirit or demon which enters the body. It must be dealt with and the evil spirit driven out. This is the function of the village shaman. In this regard Hiebert asks,

> Is it true that smallpox and pneumonia are caused by demons? Or are they caused by viruses? Or are they produced by demons in one culture and by viruses in another? And finally, how are we going to determine which explanatory model is a better picture of the 'real' world? We, in the West, might appeal to empirical facts and experiments to test these explanations. But such proof cannot be accepted so easily (1976:365).

Time, space, and causation perceptions are important to the worldview of any people. Missionaries should try to understand as much as possible of these worldview considerations. In so doing, avenues of greater understanding and communication will open up to assist the missionary in the task of evangelism and church planting.

UNDERSTANDING THE FUNCTIONS OF WORLDVIEW

For the missionary who will live and work in an alien culture the functions of worldview will be helpful tools to stimulate understanding. It is all part of the learning process which is so vital before the missionary launches out into active service. The Brewsters see it as a link with language and culture learning:

> Learning a culture is the process of learning what its people know. In a sense, learning a language, learning a culture and learning the way people think are one and the same thing in the final analysis. What is involved is 'getting inside' people's heads in order to understand how they perceive the world. To understand their knowledge, you must understand their organization of knowledge (1976:185).

Charles Kraft in his book, *Christianity in Culture*, states,

"A people's worldview is their basic model of reality" (1979: 54). In his consideration of worldview, Kraft sets forth five major functions of worldview: explanation, evaluation, reinforcement, integration, and adaptation (1979:54-56). It may be helpful to consider these functions briefly.

1. *The Explanation Function* -- This function deals with the how and why things got to be as they are. It also helps to explain how and why things will continue or change. As Kraft explains,

> If the worldview of a people conditions them
> to believe that the universe is operated by a number
> of invisible personal forces largely beyond their
> control, this will affect both their understanding
> of and their response to 'reality.' If, however,
> a people's worldview explains that the universe
> operates by means of a large number of impersonal,
> cause-and-effect operations which, if learned by
> people, can be employed by them to control the
> universe, the attitude of these people toward
> 'reality' will be much different (1979:54).

The mythology of a people, revealed in their fables, proverbs, riddles, songs, and folklore, embody these explanatory ideas. More literate and advanced societies will have science, religion, and philosophy to reveal these worldview perceptions. Basically these disciplines serve to explain why we do what we do. They provide the fundamental guidelines which people obediently follow.

2. *The Evaluation Function* -- Most societies perceive of their basic institutions, values, and goals to be the best. This is understandably national pride and it functions in all societies. In this way other people's customs and values are evaluated as being inferior or at least of lesser importance. People usually appeal to their god or gods for validation; hence, they appeal to the highest authority. Thus, it may be seen that the evaluational function of a people's worldview is an extremely vital aspect of the life of the social group.

> All important and valued behavior, whether
> of the in-group or of other groups, whether class-
> ified as economic, political, 'scientific,' social,
> educational, or whatever, is judged in terms of a
> culture's worldview assumptions, beliefs, values,
> meanings and sanctions (Kraft 1979:55).

3. *The Reinforcement Function* -- A group's worldview provides psychological reinforcement for its members. Life is made up of anxieties and crises very often; hence, a people turn to their conceptual system for encouragement or advice in these times of uncertainty. Anxiety and uncertainty often arise in connection with the life cycle. At birth, puberty, marriage, and death the worldview functions to provide the proper responses to do and say. In times of planting and harvesting, or in times of famine, hardship, or calamity the people look to their established worldview for reinforcement and solace. Sometimes a ritual or ceremony is required. This may include prayer, a trance, or some additional thinking through of the situation. In this way security and support are supplied to members of the group and they are helped to face the realities of life.

4. *The Integrative Function* -- Every group has developed means for pulling things together in a systematic way so that they all make sense. Such a system enables a people to conceptualize what reality is "and to understand and interpret all that happens day by day in this framework" (M. Kraft 1978:5). Without this integrating function life would be a puzzle with a lot of missing pieces. This integrating aspect of worldview attempts to put in the missing pieces to the puzzle. Such an integrative function is significant in any culture. As Charles Kraft states,

> Thus in its explanatory, evaluational, reinforcing, and integrating functions, worldview lies at the heart of a culture, providing the basic model (s) for bridging the gap between "objective' reality outside people's heads and the culturally agreed upon perception of that reality inside their heads (1979:56).

5. *The Adaptational Function* -- Most groups have a tendency to be conservative. But, on occasion people have been known to shift in their perceptions of reality. Changing conditions sometimes force them to think in terms which are different from their normal pattern. At such times people must be willing to adapt to new ideas and behavior patterns. It is this adaptational function that comes into play when culture change takes place. In the process of adjusting their worldviews people learn the means for resolving conflict and difficulties. This ability to adapt is an essential function of worldview. As Kraft explains, "in circumstances of cultural distortion or disequilibrium there is a resilient quality to worldview by means of which people reconcile

hitherto apparently irreconcilable differences between old
understandings and new ones" (1979:57).

WORLDVIEW BARRIERS: COMPETING RELIGIOUS SYSTEMS

When a missionary goes abroad to serve the Lord in an
alien culture and among a group of people he has not known
before, he will soon realize that significant worldview barriers exist. No group of people lives in a vacuum when it
comes to worldview. There are differing views concerning the
nature of man. For instance, the Chinese influenced by Con-
fucian thought consider man to be basically good, whereas
Euro-American groups influenced by Christian thought regard
man as a sinner in need of redemption.

The supernatural realm is a significant one, and the missionary must seek to understand the supernatural perceptions
of the people to whom he goes with the Good News.

To communicate a new message effectively it
is first necessary to understand the organized
knowledge which people already have about supernatural matters. As you become aware of the
categories that people already have, you can better
communicate your message in clear understandable
ways (Brewster & Brewster 1976:212).

These categories referred to above are found in the worldviews of the group. In thinking in terms of worldview barriers it is helpful to consider the theory of natural groupings and to realize that alien worldview assumptions lead to
different conclusions.

The Theory of Natural Groupings

In attempting to look at the peoples of the world the
anthropologist is impressed with the great diversity of
peoples. There are so many groups. Each group has distinc-
tives which are a part of their identity. When each group
is studied carefully a specific worldview emerges which serves
to guide people through life and to provide a sense of meaning
and purpose. Each group will have a norm or norms which sets
forth its basic guidelines. Mayers notes, "The norm of any
social group equals the sum total of its values, norms, expectations, rules, and aspirations" (1974:82). Outsiders
coming into the group will need to take time to learn the
norm of the group. This, of course, takes time and will be a
part of language and culture learning. Nevertheless, the

missionary must not expect the worldview of an alien group to be the same or even similar to his own.

The theory of natural groupings simply recognizes that the world is composed of many different groups of people. That they have a right to exist and to be regarded as valid societies should be a part of the missionary's basic approach. Such an approach will affirm the validity of other cultural groups and provide a platform of mutual respect as the missionary seeks to identify with the host culture.

Alien Worldview Assumptions Lead to Different Conclusions

As soon as the diversity of cultural groupings is recognized, it will become apparent that other worldviews will be identified. The way people perceive the universe and its functions will vary considerable. Charles Kraft comments in this regard:

> We assume that the natural universe is predictable, and understandable, and scientifically describable. We therefore attempt to understand and describe the causes, or at least the factors involved in such phenomena as storms (and weather in general), sickness and health, misfortune and success. If something happens we are determined to at least find out how it happened, whether or not we can explain why. . . But the people of other cultures start from other assumptions concerning the universe, and of course, come out with very different conclusions (1979:58).

Within the animist of tribal worldview the universe seems quite mysterious. If a tragedy or calamity occurs, it is due to the whim or displeasure of a personal spirit. Consequently, this spirit must be appeased. This worldview is vastly different from that of the missionary and often appears to stand in the way as a huge barrier.

The way Buddhists and Hindus look at life is quite different from our Euro-American perspective. Nida comments:

> In Buddhism, for example, ultimate meaning is to be found in escape from this world of delusion, and hence by transfering 'real meaning' out of the world of people and things, one can readily make sense out of the anomalies of existence. In Hinduism, aggression, based on ethnic

conflict, froze the social structure to the
benefit of the ruling castes, but still left
some ray of hope for the meaning of life in
providing ultimate escape into the world soul of
of Brahman. Cruelly enough, however, this   g
meaning could be attained only by means of a
ritual system completely controlled by the
priestly Brahman caste (1968:9).

Other religious systems could be mentioned, like Confucianism, Taoism, Islam, Shintoism, and many more. The
peoples who espouse these religions possess distinctive
worldviews. For the missionary attempting to introduce the
Good News of Jesus Christ these worldviews loom in the way
as barriers. They will have to be studied individually, and
only then may strategies for evangelism be employed to introduce the Christian message. David R. Hesselgrave's, *Communicating Christ Cross-Culturally* (1978), Part III, contains
a very helpful discussion directly related to this topic of
worldview.

UNDERSTANDING THE SIGNIFICANCE OF SYMBOLS

Every cultural group has devised symbolic reference as a
tool and an aid for giving meaning and purpose to life.
Symbols help to communicate basic values to other members of
the group. In chapter three we have discussed language and
culture as symbolic systems. In considering symbols we shall
look at the nature of symbols and their limitations. Also,
it will be helpful to note how presuppositions affect interpretation of symbols, and how symbols relate to Christian
communication.

The Nature of Symbols

Symbols are labels we use to identify concepts. A symbol
can be used quite apart from its immediate context or stimuli.
Symbols relate to worldview in that they reflect the ideas
and values of the system of which they are a part. A
Japanese torii, a Buddhist image, a wooden cross, a pair of
chopsticks, are symbols of reality to members of groups which
employ them in their worldview. Each culture orders its own
symbols to best meet its needs. As Keesing observes,

A culture, as we bring its patterning to
light, is fantastically intricate, a web of inter-
locked symbols and meanings on many levels. An
element--whether it is a design for house entrances,

a ritual procedure, or a dress style--is
limited not only by physical possibilities,
but also by the 'rules' of symbolic ordering
in the culture (1971:315).

Religion is a valid part of culture, and both religion
and culture possess symbols. Donald Flatt notes that, "religion is concerned with a people's worldview, their cosmo-
logical ideas, but not in a philosophical sense, in isolation from the rest of life. Religion is concerned with the
worldview in relation to human character and conduct" (1973:
336). In many societies it is obvious that religious symbolism permeates every aspect of life. Birth, puberty,
marriage, death, planting, and harvesting all have religious
significance which is symbolized in various ways. Platt
states that, "Religious symbols, so long as they are in
current and active use, both reflect and impose a system of
concepts and values which characterize a given society and
dictate its major cultural configuration" (1973:335-336).

The Limitation of Symbols

Symbols are very helpful vehicles for conveying meaning
within a cultural system. There are also limitations to
their use. In this regard Nida observes,

> One of the basic facts about symbols is that
> they are both useful and difficult to use; that
> they both reveal and obscure. On the one hand,
> they reveal truth, for they help us to identify,
> explore, and interchange conceptions; but they
> also obscure, for they have the pernicious ten-
> dency to be slippery, never meaning just one
> thing but several things, not standing for a
> definite object by symbolizing a conception.
> Since these symbols as the 'playthings of the
> mind' seem to stand for reality, we tend to
> think that they are reality. And in the end, we
> deceive ourselves into thinking that if a person
> can recite the doctrines, then he must assur-
> edly have experienced what these doctrines des-
> cribe (1960:69).

Such misuse of symbols can easily lead to hypocrisy. It is
somehow easier for people to conform verbally than morally.
A Christian worldview which integrates doctrine and practice
is much to be preferred.

Cultural Differences Affect Symbol Interpretation

The worldview of the recipients of the Scriptures is quite different from our worldview in the twentieth century; hence, we have problems interpreting scripture. For example, we consider a fox to be a sly and cunning animal. When Jesus refers to Herod as a fox in Luke 13:32, we automatically think He meant sly. Yet, in Hebrew cultural agreement the term was intended to indicate treachery. The book *Peace Child* (1974), by Don Richardson, tells of the New Guinea Sawi people admiring the treachery of Judas. To them he was the hero of the New Testament and not Jesus. Charles Kraft comments:

> A much bigger problem of interpretation lies in those areas where the Scriptures use cultural symbols that are different. We are tempted to interpret according to what seems to be the 'plain meaning'--as if we could get the proper meaning of Scripture as we would from a document originally written in English. To avoid this pitfall, many translation theorists are now contending that a faithful translation of the Scriptures must involve enough interpretation to protect the reader from being seriously misled at points such as these (1979:132).

Thus, it may be seen that worldview considerations and cultural backgrounds of people are extremely important. Misunderstandings can arise easily if the missionary is not careful in the interpretation of symbols.

Symbols and Christian Communication

The use of symbols is an integral part of the communication process. "A culture can be viewed as the symbol systems, such as languages, rituals, gestures and objects, that people create in order to think and communicate" (Hiebert 1976b:47). Crosscultural communication sometimes has its difficulties, but it is possible to establish effective communication between persons of different cultural backgrounds. Nida notes that there are three principal reasons for this fact:

> (1) the processes of human reasoning are essentially the same, irrespective of cultural diversity; (2) all peoples have a common range of human experience, and (3) all peoples possess

the capacity for at least some adjustment to
the symbolic 'grids' of others (1960:90).

A good understanding of worldview and cultural backgrounds becomes a challenging goal for the missionary who
would be effective as a communicator. The message the missionary bears is worthy of his best efforts to communicate
it well. In this regard Nida comments:

> If the communication of the Christian
> message is to be culturally meaningful, in
> terms of the total lives of the people, certain
> features are essential: (1) it must use meaning-
> ful indigenous symbols wherever any concepts are
> crucial and (2) the implications of the message
> must be explained in concrete terms which are
> culturally applicable within a given society
> (Smalley 1978:841).

The presuppositions of a people--a vital part of world-
view--will affect the interpretation and understanding of
the message. Missionaries need to be aware of basic presuppositions held by the people among whom they live and
work. Nida shares a humorous illustration of what can
happen:

> During a devotional period after breakfast a
> missionary in Yucatan was trying to explain to an
> Indian servant what it meant to possess the Spirit
> of God--in itself a highly complex concept. He
> attempted to put his point across by saying, 'If
> the Spirit of God enters into your heart, what do
> you have in your heart?' To which the woman an-
> swered, 'I do not know.' (After all, she was not
> used to thinking in terms of spirits in her heart.)
> The missionary then tried to make his point by
> picking up a glass from the breakfast table and
> asking the woman, 'If I put water in this glass,
> what would I have in it?' To which the woman re-
> plied, 'Milk!' At first the missionary was dis-
> mayed at what seemed to be a failure in the most
> elementary logic. A guest who was present re-
> minded him that each morning at breakfast he, the
> missionary, had put some powdered milk into the
> glass, whereupon the servant woman had been asked
> to pour in some water. The result was not water,
> but milk. The earlier misunderstanding between
> the missionary and the servant was not the result

of differences in logical processes of reasoning,
but in what the two had started with: he with an
empty glass and she with one having powdered
milk in it. Whenever two persons fail to communicate effectively, it is not necessarily because of any superiority or inferiority of reasoning processes, but rather because the two
begin with different presuppositions (1960:91).

SUMMARY

Worldview is vitally important to any group. The ways
of perceiving the world are many. The nature and function
of worldview need to be understood by the missionary. The
way in which a particular people view the world around them
will affect the way they will interpret the Gospel. Since
worldview considerations pertain to the areas of time, space,
causation, the supernatural, and interpersonal relationships,
almost every aspect of life is affected by it.

As the missionary understands more of worldview, many of
the basic cultural assumptions of the people will be unlocked
and revealed. Worldview barriers may be expected. They
usually reveal themselves in the form of a religious system.
An understanding of worldview will enable the missionary to
hurdle such barriers and begin to communicate more effectively
on a wave length which is relevant and understandable by the
people.

Since a culture may be viewed as a series of symbol systems such as languages, cultures, gestures, and objects
which people produce in order to think and communicate, these
systems are important keys for the missionary to use in order
to unlock doors for communication. This whole subject of
worldview is no light matter. It has many ramifications. It
demands the serious study and understanding on the part of
missionaries if they wish to communicate effectively.

How can the missionary learn about worldview? First of
all, he should be sure to take courses in cultural anthropology and cross-cultural communication as a part of his missionary preparation for the field. Secondly, he should read
widely obtaining any published ethnographies of the people
among whom he will live and work. A third source of information will be the writings of field missionaries who have
been working in isolated areas among groups of people about
whom little or nothing has been written. Field missionaries
should be encouraged to do original field research in the

area of worldview, write it up, and publish it for the benefit of others. In these ways missionaries may be learning
about and contributing to the literature on worldview.

7

The Need to Understand
the Dynamics of Cultural Change

Since the missionary will be involved in the process of
culture change, it is imperative that he understand the dynamics of culture change. It is helpful to note as a starting point that no culture stands still. Cultures all over
the world are always in the process of changing. "One of
the most important subdivisions of cultural anthropology is
cultural dynamics, concerned with processes and conditions
of cultural stability and change" (Taylor 1973:497). On the
other hand, anthropologists have found that all cultures resist rapid change, and they are challenged to investigate
the reasons for this stability. This is an extremely fascinating area of study for the missionary. Its importance
is great concerning the success or failure of missionary
endeavor. It will be helpful to consider the clash between
tradition and change, the process of innovation, the missionary as a change agent, the significance of cross-cultural conversion, and the importance of contextualization of
the Christian message.

THE CLASH BETWEEN TRADITION AND CHANGE

Anthropologists have found that societies everywhere tend
to make every effort to maintain the status quo. Yet, it is
a fact of life that change is always taking place.

The Fact of Change

Sometimes change takes place very imperceptibly. "No
group of people, whether primitive or civilized, has a

completely static culture, for everything is subject to and
in the process of change" (Nida 1954:225).

The world around us is constantly changing. Consider the
giant strides made in the fields of technology, transportation, communication, and education. If we compare these
areas in 1980 with our grandparents' era of the 1920's, we
are staggered by the rapid and sigificant advances. Today
the impact of civilization upon non-literate societies worldwide is considerable. It is common to find animistic tribes-
people in the mountains of North Thailand living in bamboo
and grass-roofed houses but with a Japanese transistor radio
blaring out rock music! Eskimos and Indians of northern
Canada and the northwest now ride snowmobiles to check their
trap lines instead of the traditional dog team and sled.
Actually, tribal societies have been undergoing continual
change long before modern ideas and technology arrived. Cultural change has been a constant of culture, and anthropologists are interested in understanding how and when it takes
place. We must accept change as a fact of life. Missionaries have a part in culture change since they have a way of
importing Western culture wherever they go. Reyburn noted
this fact when he wrote:

> . . . the missionary carries Western culture
> with him and communicates it whether he wants to
> or not. This is so even if the communication of
> Western thought forms comes across as nonsense
> and confusion to the native. The missionary who
> disavows being a carrier of Western culture is
> denying himself the very structure of his thought
> in which he cradles his presentation of the gos-
> pel and life (Smalley 1978:512).

Resistance to Change

Resistance to change may be expected from the older generation within any societal group. They prefer the well-
worn and familiar ways; hence, new ideas and customs become
automatically suspect. "'We know that the younger people
will abandon our way,' remarked an old San Blas chieftain,
as he lamented the rapid changes which were being introduced
into the islands by school teachers, traders, missionaries,
and politicians" (Nida 1954:224).

The elders and leaders of any group feel it their responsibility to protect and preserve the cultural ways of
the group. Thus, it is only natural to expect a measure of

resistance to culture change.

> There are few cultures where the elders do
> not disapprove of the departures of the young
> from the traditions of an earlier generation,
> or where the young people do not deviate in
> some respect from certain forms of behavior
> approved by the older people . . . . that their
> opposition to change is, however, ineffectual,
> is a lesson that seems never to be learned
> (Herskovits 1967:142).

Change may be hindered or retarded by the older generation;
nevertheless, it will take place continually over a period
of many years. Sometimes it will take place rapidly, and at
other times almost imperceptibly. Change is indeed a significant fact of life. It is a vital aspect of cultural
dynamics.

Incentives for Change

What are some of the incentives to origination and change?
The incentives will vary from group to group and from place
to place. A desire for prestige can be an incentive. If the
people see that a new custom or way of doing things will give
them greater prestige, they will opt for it. Reyburn recounts an African illustration of how the desire for prestige may result in sacrifice and pain:

> A postparturient mother at the Batouri
> mission hospital, the wife of an evolue, sat
> feeding her newborn babe from a baby bottle while
> her breasts painfully dripped with milk. She was
> willing to endure the physical pain in order to
> maintain her social distance from the common
> village women who would never dare take the
> privilege of bottle feeding (Smalley 1978:516).

Release from tension may be another incentive. When
people observe that the new way of doing things contributes
to a lessening of tension, they will want to change for that
very reason.

"Another condition stimulating change is deprivation, defined by Barnett as the elimination of something people feel
they have a right to" (Taylor 1973:509).

The desire to have more or less of something is closely

related, and it too, will provide an incentive for change.
The desire to create may well be another incentive. Often
new tools and methodologies will stimulate people to become
creative and their fellow men may adopt their new tools and
new ways.

A desire to gain relief from boredom and monotony may
become an incentive for change as well. In many cases the
introduction of transistor radios and television may be
classed in this category. Some people have not only adopted
these media, but they have become addicted to them. As a
result their lifestyles have changed considerably and not
always for the better.

Stability and Change

Stability and change are vital factors which have challenged anthropologists for years. The reasons behind these
factors continue to stimulate much research even today.
"Conservatism and change in culture are the result of the
interplay of environmental, historical, and psychological
factors. All must be considered when studies of cultural
processes are made" (Herskovits 1967:149). Many factors are
involved in culture change. This is one of the reasons why
culture change is such a fascinating field of study. It is
this consideration which makes it mandatory for the missionary to understand his/her role as a catalyst for change.

> Culture change and, for that matter, cul-
> tural stability, are viewed as the result of
> many thousands of individual choices. In making
> choices, members of a society take into account
> the expectations of others and the probable con-
> sequences of their own conformity or deviance.
> Some choices are made almost automatically and
> unconsciously, while others may require extensive
> consultation, soul-searching, and emotional up-
> heaval (Bock 1974:203).

Geographic proximity to large cities is a major factor in the rate of culture change. New ideas come from the
big cities and these are disseminated to smaller cities,
towns and ultimately to the villages. Remoteness from larger
centers will slow culture change considerably. Cultural
stability will not be threatened greatly in such remote settings. Change will come eventually, but its progress will be
more gradual than in the large cities where change takes
place most rapidly.

> We may not be able to predict exactly
> what a specific individual will do in a given
> situation, but the behavioral sciences are
> rapidly improving their ability to predict
> the behavior of groups; and it is the changing
> pattern of individual choices within a group
> which in the long run determines the direction
> of culture change (Bock 1974:203).

There will always be a measure of tension between tradition
and change. This is what makes culture dynamic. "Change,
then, is a universal cultural phenomenon, and the processes
of change over a period of time constitute the dynamics of
culture" (Herskovits 1967:144).

THE PROCESS OF INNOVATION

Innovation is a process. Many variables are involved in
stimulating and affecting culture change. According to
Barnett (1953:61) one of these "is the desire for change or
non-desire of a person or group of persons." Other factors
are involved as well. In considering the process of innovation let us look at the role of ideas, the role of the
advocate, the basic stages in innovation, some risks with
innovation, and variables affecting acceptance and rejection.

The Role of Ideas

In order for a new custom or behavior pattern to be
accepted someone must first have an idea. It may come out of
a felt need, or it may be something another person observed
while visiting another city or town. Innovation often consists of recombining previous ideas in new ways. Homer
Barnett (1953) has written extensively regarding the innovation of new ideas and how a receptor people react to them.
Kraft asks the question:

> How is an ideology communicated across
> cultures? First of all, it must be recognized,
> as Homer Barnett convincingly points out: (1)
> that all cultural change is at base the result
> of changes in ideas; (2) that all cultural
> changes are initiated by individuals; (3) that,
> therefore, the laws of cultural change are psy-
> chological laws (1974:305).

In many cultures of the world missionaries played a leading role in introducing new ideas. In the process Western

technology and influences followed. These were communicated, perhaps unintentionally, but nonetheless communicated.

> Missionary endeavor has had effects com-
> parable to the commercial activities of traders.
> Because it also represents an effort to extend
> the range of one system of ideas at the expense
> of another, it has highlighted contrasts in cus-
> toms, not infrequently, with innovative conse-
> quences. The penetration of Christian mission-
> aries into remote parts of the world comes to
> mind in this connection (Barnett 1953:47).

The Role of the Advocate

While new ideas are essential to culture change, it is also important who is advocating change. How new ideas are presented and by whom is an important consideration. The term "advocate" refers to the one desiring to introduce the new idea or custom. The term "innovator" is usually re-served for the insider within the culture. Kraft helpfully explains this relationship:

> . . . in ideological change one must dis-
> tinguish between the role of the acceptor or
> innovator and that of the advocate of innovation.
> Though most change is recommended by persons
> within a culture to others within the culture,
> the advocate, the person who recommends a change,
> may come from outside the culture--that is, from
> another culture. The innovator, the person who
> actually affects the recommended change, however,
> may not--he is always an insider. It is, there-
> fore, the task of any outsider who advocates a
> change of ideology to convince someone (s) with-
> in the culture of the desirability of a change.
> He must win that person or those persons over
> to his point of view (1974:305-306).

The importance of being a good advocate is great. This responsibility highlights the necessity for the missionary to become an insider as quickly as possible. Nevertheless, his white skin and foreign ways will always mark him as an outsider in the host society. The need for adequate language and culture learning will readily be apparent. These are vital steps toward the goal of becoming an effective com-municator of the Good News.

Basic Stages in Innovation

Hiebert refers to three steps in innovation: "Analysis, identification, and substitution are the three basic stages in innovation. People are constantly making such substitutions, although they are often unaware that they are doing so" (1976:425). People who feel the need for change first analyze their present situation. Deprivation may be a factor in this analysis, or there may be a felt need for improvement. Once this need is identified, then something may be done to meet that need. It is here that the third stage, substitution, is employed. Sometimes there are options to choose from; thus, substitutions may be selected to meet the need.

I recall visiting a Hutterite colony in southern Saskatchewan over a period of several years. In each of my earlier visits I noted the presence of outdoor toilets close to the living quarters of the residents. On my last visit I was invited into one of the apartments where the proud occupants displayed a shiny, brand new bathroom, complete with molded combination tub and shower. The Hutterites had done some analyzing. They felt a need to avoid the icy cold Saskatchewan winters in favor of a nice warm bathroom. They merely substituted an indoor toilet for an outdoor one--something thousands had done long before they had. While they were at it, they combined the facility for bathing as well. Here was an innovation which brought about a measure of culture change. "People feel the pressures of culture in two ways: as a press, which prescribes certain kinds of behavior, and as a pull which prescribes and enculturates other thoughts and actions" (Hiebert 1976:433).

Risks With Innovation

Those who desire change always run the risk of uncertainty concerning the innovations which they may wish to introduce. Yet, this is another vital aspect of cultural dynamics. The innovator must be willing to take the risk. Lyle Schaller comments in this regard:

Peter Drucker has identified three major risks in innovation. The first is that it will make obsolete current practices and patterns of operation. The second is that it will fail. The third is that it will succeed--but in succeeding it may produce unforeseen consequences that create new problems. A simple contemporary

illustration of this is the local church that
deliberately adopts an innovative approach to
ministering to young persons. When these
efforts do succeed they frequently produce a
deep sense of hostility and alienation among
members in the thirty to fifty-five age range
(1972:54).

It is in being willing to take risks that innovation
takes place. Often it takes much time and repeated efforts
before an innovation is accepted. When the Gospel is introduced it must be remembered that the innovations which it
brings may be far greater than the missionary realizes. It
is at this point that the ministry of the Holy Spirit is
vital; however, an understanding of cultural dynamics will
be extremely helpful.

Variables Affecting Acceptance and Rejection

Robert Taylor has summarized twelve variables which have
a bearing on the acceptance or rejection of innovations.
These factors differ from people to people; nevertheless,
they are significant issues to keep in mind regarding culture change. Missionaries will gain valuable insights from
Taylor's (1973:515) suggestions in the following ways:
1. "Objectification is a necessary prerequisite to acceptance, for a custom cannot be accepted by a respondent
   who has not observed an action, artifact, or utterance
   which expresses the custom." Any new innovation must be
   introduced by someone. Such a person or persons objectify
   the new custom so that others in the group see and understand what it is. Such objectification is a beginning
   point for innovation.
2. "Advocacy may also be a determining factor. Someone has
   to advocate the innovation." The one who introduces the
   innovation becomes the advocate. As a result of his role
   in such advocacy others will be influenced to accept the
   innovation.
3. "Personality is often of great importance--customs may be
   rejected if the objectifier's personality is offensive."
   Missionaries will want to be sensitive as to how they are
   being perceived by the receptor people. Their very personalities may well influence how a people will accept the
   message that they bring.
4. "Personal relations comprise another variable often of
   importance. It refers particularly to friendship and
   kinship." Here is where the importance of family, relatives, and friendships play a significant role in

spreading new customs or innovations. If an advocate has relatives or close friends in a town or village, this factor may influence others to accept the Gospel.

5. "Majority affiliation is, for many respondents, a recommendation for acceptance." For example, if more than one half of a village or town embrace the Gospel, their majority expression of faith will recommend the Christian message to the others who are unbelievers.

6. "Compatibility is a cultural factor of considerable importance in understanding a respondent's reaction." If the innovation is perceived to be incompatible within the sociocultural value structure, it will not be readily accepted. However, if it is indeed compatible, its acceptance will be more rapid. This is a sensitive area for the missionary to evaluate.

7. "Efficiency is frequently a factor recommending acceptance." If a new custom or innovation demonstrates efficiency and people recognize its value, this will certainly aid acceptance.

8. "Cost is one of the commonest deterrents to acceptance." Underdeveloped countries with large numbers of illiterates will not be able to spend large sums of money for new innovations. This is a practical factor which must be understood when introducing new customs which may cost money to buy and maintain among the receptor people.

9. "Penalty, of a necessary concomitant of acceptance, may influence the respondent to reject a custom." If it is against the law of the land to become a Christian, or if it means being rejected and cast off by one's family, then such penalties will influence people to reject the Gospel. Conditions in some Muslim countries today are severe; hence, this affects the spread of the Christian message.

10. "Advantage is another factor of widespread significance. Some peoples have overtly accepted Christianity to acquire the material benefits available from missionaries." Missions who specialize in medical and educational work have found that these ministries often influence people to accept the Christian message. Among lower classes of very poor people such advantages may become motivating factors in leading them to become Christians. Missionaries need to be aware of these factors.

11. "Mastery of custom is a significant determinant of a respondent's reaction." If a new custom may be easily mastered and utilized by a people, their acceptance of it may be rapid and wholehearted; however, if mastery is difficult or virtually impossible, their reaction may be one of rejection.

12. "Functional repercussions may result in rejection."

Should a new custom or innovation cause disturbance and strong reaction among the people, such a repercussion may lead to rejection. Missionaries will want to be very careful regarding the way in which new ideas and customs are introduced. Avoiding adverse repercussions will aid acceptance.

In seeking to understand the importance of these variables in their relationship to innovation the role of anthropology is very useful. A. R. Tippett, both a missionary and an anthropologist, comments regarding this kind of usefulness (1973:122).

It also shows us the difference between effective and ineffective relationships of the advocate to the acceptor. It shows us what kind of advocacy is likely to meet with obstruction and rejection or acceptance. In other words, the anthropologist can tell us many things about how the gospel might be more effectively presented.

THE MISSIONARY AS AN AGENT OF CHANGE

The average Christian does not commonly think of the missionary as an agent of change, but in a real sense he or she is such an agent. Wherever the Gospel has been proclaimed change has taken place. In some areas of the world the changes have been greater than in other areas. It will be helpful to consider the missionary role in this regard, understanding culture as a system, and the Gospel and change.

The Missionary Role

Most Christians conceive of missionaries as evangelists, pastors, and teachers. Or, they think also of missionary doctors, nurses, and medical technicians. They focus mainly on the biblical, spiritual, and service dimensions of the missionary task. This is quite understandable. It is true that the missionary is an evangelist who proclaims the Good News. Also, when a group of people have believed in Christ, he teaches them and acts as their pastor, at least for a temporary period until national pastors can be trained for the task. While these roles are all well and good, there is another aspect which may easily be overlooked. I refer to the role of the missionary as an agent of change in areas other than religion.

"Historically, the missionary, in stride with the European

trader and colonial administrator, has been an important agent
of culture change in non-western societies" (Whiteman 1974:17).
Many countries of Africa, Asia, and elsewhere have benefited
immensely from change instituted by medical and educational
missionaries. Culture change has been stimulated economically,
socially, and educationally as a result. For the most part
this type of change has been received thankfully and Christianity has been widely recognized as a religion concerned for
social as well as for religious matters. In order to fulfill
the missionary task the missionary must be involved with
people as an agent of change. As Mayers (1974:281) notes,
some missionaries have feelings of ambivalence regarding their
role.

> The missionary admittedly sees himself as an
> agent of change. Because he's been told so often
> that affecting change is not his prerogative, he
> may feel guilty about his role, but he need't be,
> because without contributing to change there can
> be no fulfilling of the Great Commission.

Since the missionary's role includes many aspects of culture change, it is imperative that he or she understand the
systemic nature of change. Culture functions as a system.
Change in one aspect of culture usually affects other areas
as well. These relationships must be carefully understood.

Understanding Culture as a System

The anthropologists Malinowski and Radcliffe-Brown con-
tributed to our understanding of culture change. Their names
have been associated with the concept of functionalism. Prior
to their time, other anthropologists were studying unrelated
customs and traits from a wide range of sources. The func-
tionalist school began to look at different aspects of culture as parts of an intricate system. They believed and
taught that culture was systemic in nature. This was an important concept for missionaries to understand in their work
among peoples from many cultural backgrounds. "The agent of
change must know the system of the culture before he can
effectively participate in its change. Otherwise, he will
introduce those ways that derive from his own way of life,
but these may never meet the need of the target culture"
(Mayers 1974:92).

In chapter one the need for the missionary to understand
the nature of culture was stressed. This is an important
part of missionary preparation, and it relates to the systemic
nature of culture.

nature of culture.

> One of the elementary principles of change,
> but one difficult to get across to many change
> agents, is the fact that the customs which com-
> prise a culture are linked to one another and to
> elements of the cultural field. The fact that
> cultures are systems and that modifications of
> parts of a culture may have destructive reper-
> cussions to the goals of the change agent or
> those of the people undergoing change often
> goes unappreciated until serious harm is done
> (Taylor 1973:517).

Sad to say, some missionaries have gone forth with the idea
that their chief aim is simply to "win souls" to Christ.
Often they have not stopped to realize that the people--the
"souls"--are not mere disembodied spirits, but valid persons
who exist in distinct groups comprising numerous societies
around the world. These groups experience meaning, purpose
and relevance as they live out their group identity. It is
at this very juncture that an understanding of anthropological
principles is so essential before the missionary commences
cross-cultural ministry. The systemic nature of a group of
people must be understood. It is vital to the success of
missionary endeavor. Mayers sees the task of the missionary
clearly when he writes:

> He must first of all see the society he is
> entering as composed of persons organized into
> an intricate system of human relationships, inter-
> acting through that society's institutions. Each
> society is a valid, integrated whole, organized
> according to a system of hierarchical levels. To
> change behavior on any level of such a system will
> result in reverberating consequences throughout
> the entire society-as-system and will result in
> the necessity for related and reinforcing changes
> above and below the actual level of the hierarchy
> initially changed, if disintegration throughout
> the entire society is to be avoided (1974:281).

These considerations are vital to missionary work and
relationships with national Christians. For the missionary
not to be equipped for ministry in a cross-cultural context
is unthinkable in the contemporary world. Every effort should
be made to gain a cross-cultural perspective before embarking
upon missionary service.

The Gospel and Cultural Change

The Gospel message is primarily a spiritual message, but
it is communicated to human beings. The nature of the Gospel
message is such that it radically affects mankind and their
cultural systems. Behavior patterns are influenced as well.
In the African context the issues of polygamy and ancestor
worship have been tension issues ever since the Gospel was
introduced on that continent. These institutions must be
understood within their own cultural systems first of all.
Culture change may well come, but the way in which it comes
is extremely important. Change should be introduced within
the cultural system by the nationals who understand the system.
God, the Holy Spirit, is able to guide national Christians
even as He guides Christians from the West. Missionaries
must not force culture change upon the people. Change occurs
most readily when it is instigated by insiders who understand
their system, rather than by outsiders who have much to learn.

Missionaries need to be trained to differentiate the
Christian message from that which is cultural. If not, difficulties and misunderstandings easily arise. Darrell Whiteman, writing from a New Guinea perspective, states,

> Thus, even though the missionary is
> attempting to proclaim a message whose emphasis
> is upon a radical change for every follower,
> thus cutting across cultural distinctions, his
> inability to separate the essential principles
> of Christianity from their expression in his own
> cultural framework, causes him to disseminate a
> message that is very confusing at best, since it
> is expressed in the cultural tradition of the
> missionary rather than in the cultural idiom
> with which a New Guinean can identify (1974:28).

It becomes very easy for one group to impose its own language and cultural ways upon another group. This may be done
quite unconsciously by the domineering group. Sometimes it
is accomplished during the course of missionary work. Barnett
offers an excellent illustration:

> Inevitably native immigrant converts like
> the Samoans and Fijians have imported certain
> elements of their culture into the new lands
> where they have taken up residence. Keesing
> reports that Tahitian missionaries in prosely-
> tizing other islanders have used their native

> tongue so exclusively that their converts now
> speak Tahitian rather than their own language
> (1953:311).

Cultural imperialism should be avoided. Memories of the colonial past do not dissipate their influence easily. Identification with the host people and culture is an essential.
Good missionaries make every effort to identify well with the
people and their cultural system.

THE SIGNIFICANCE OF CONVERSION IN A CROSS-CULTURAL CONTEXT

Christian conversion is a significant issue in missions.
In a cross-cultural setting it may easily become very complex
and have far reaching implications. In considering this concept we shall first ask what is Christian conversion? Then,
we'll note several anthropological problems, look at conversion as a process, and finally consider the "Engel scale"
(The Spiritual-Decision Process).

What is Christian Conversion?

Theologically considered, Christian conversion is the work
of God within the life of a non-believer causing him to turn
from his sin and to believe in Jesus Christ as Savior and Lord
in order to become a responsible member of His church. This is
a faith commitment which entails an allegiance to Jesus Christ
alone. Conversion is not the work of the evangelist, but it
is a work of the Holy Spirit of God. The task of the evangelist
is to provide the necessary information about the Good News.

> Christian mission then might be classified
> by the anthropologist as culture change by directed
> advocacy. We must recognize, of course, that this
> is to consider it from the human point of view.
> There is a divine side. We realize that God is at
> work in the situation; that in the last analysis
> it is God who converts people; that we men can
> never 'save' anyone or make them into new creatures.
> Science and psychology have not yet explained the
> precise nature of that change in man when he is
> converted. It is observable but unexplained
> change (Tippett 1973:122).

Here in North America it is the commonly accepted pattern
for persons to make an individual commitment to Christ. However, in other parts of the world people prefer to make group
decisions. These distinct groups have adopted a form of

social organization which knits the people together with a
strong sense of solidarity. Their group orientation is so
tight that departure from or alternatives in their system are
not allowable without the consent of the recognized leadership within the group. In tribal societies this leadership
may be composed of the chief or headman and his council of
senior advisors. In other groups their particular hierarchy
of leadership must be consulted before any form of culture
change is permitted. Often within such systems the religious
practitioners are considered ranking persons of influence in
decision-making. They are always consulted regarding issues
which affect the group. Thus, when it comes to introducing
the Christian message, the religious hierarchy may feel
threatened if a new religion is being promulgated among the
people.

In the Far East among the Chinese and Japanese peoples
there is a strong emphasis upon family relationships. Loy-
alty to family ranks high on the hierarchy of group values.
In some such groups even the selection of a marriage partner
is arranged by the parents--not by "boy-meets-girl-fall-in-
love" syndrome which is so common in North America. This
pattern may appear shocking to North Americans, but it is
considered the norm and quite acceptable in many cultures.
In a group with a social organization like this it is unthinkable that a young person should affirm an allegiance to
Jesus Christ in direct opposition to the expectations of the
family who may be loyal to Confucianism, Buddhism, or Shintoism. Individual decision-making in matters of such magnitude
is simply not permitted. The dynamics of the culture do not
allow a person to exercise any such liberty or individuality.
Some young persons have been driven out of their own homes by
irate parents who were greatly distressed because of a son or
daughter making a decision for Christ.

From his personal experience during many years of missionary service in Oceania, A. R. Tippett (1977:204) observes,
"Most of the Oceanic peoples who have become Christian have
done so by group movements. . . They are multi-individual movements." In such cases the elders of the group will discuss
the decision to believe or not to believe in Christ and come
to a joint consensus. When this consensus has been reached,
the decision to become Christians will be made as a group.
Each individual in the group will believe in Jesus Christ, but
they choose to do so as a unit. This pattern of decision-
making is different for North Americans; hence, they must
attempt to understand the decision-making ways of the people
among whom they live and serve.

Anthropological Problems

Tippett suggests that the study of group conversion involves a number of anthropological problems: (1) the problem
of advocacy; (2) the problem of meaning; (3) the problem of
incorporation (1977:204). The problem of advocacy has to do
with the possibility of either acceptance or rejection by the
group. They should be free to accept or reject of their own
free will.

The problem of meaning relates to cross-cultural communication. Can the missionary be sure that the meaning he in-
tends is received and understood by the receptor people?
"That is, we assume that it means the same thing to us as it
does to the acceptor-rejector. In reality cultural, linguistic or situational factors may give it a different meaning,
and a misunderstanding results" (Tippett 1973:127).

The problem of incorporation relates to a people leaving
their old ways and entering the new way. This transition
must be symbolized and made real for them. It has to do
with belonging because people like to know who they are and
where they belong. Tippett explains it this way:

> When there is a people-movement out of paganism,
> and the people involved burn their fetishes, or
> destroy their sacred groves, or bury their skull
> trophies, or cast their sacred paraphernalia into
> the sea as a symbol of their cutting themselves
> off from paganism, it is important that they
> should not be left as people who do not belong to
> anything (1973:128-129).

Some missions have been known to keep people waiting many
months or even years before receiving baptism. This is usually done because they want to teach the people the full
significance of what it means to be a Christian. In the meantime the people are left dangling wondering who they are and
where they belong. This could be disastrous and lead to
reversion on the part of some. Other missions have practiced
baptism soon after the commitment to believe in order to incorporate the people. Then they teach the Word and explain
the meaning to the people as growing Christians. This whole
procedure leads us to consider the process of conversion.

Conversion as a Process

It is most helpful to consider conversion as a process.

A. R. Tippett has developed a model showing how the process of decision takes place.

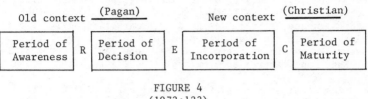

FIGURE 4
(1973:123)

During the period of awareness the people are hearing the Good News and beginning to grasp its meaning. Over a period of time they reach the point of realization, "R," and the Gospel becomes relevant. In thinking of groups from Oceania, they consider the option to believe or reject Christ. This period may take many months or spread over a year before they reach the point of encounter, "E." This phase may be marked by fetish-burning or the destruction of demon things. "Finally, there needs to be some act of incorporation whereby the decision-making process is consummated by bringing the group into the Christian community so they know who they are and where they belong in the new context" (Tippett 1973: 123).

In the April, 1977 issue of *Missiology* Tippett modified his diagram to include the last phase which he called the "period of maturity." He explains it like this:

> 'C' is the point of consummation (or con-
> firmation), where people, having been incor-
> porated in the fellowship group and having
> learned to use the 'means of grace' and to study
> the Scriptures, and so forth, now pass on into
> a deepening experience of faith, 'growing in
> grace' or sanctification (1977:219).

Seeing the process of conversion in a graphic way can be helpful in understanding how that wonderful work of grace unfolds.

The Engel Scale

The Engel scale was first published in *Church Growth Bulletin* in 1973, and later in James Engel's and H. Wilbert Norton's book, *What's Gone Wrong With the Harvest?* (1975). The rudimentary forms of this scale were developed by a

Danish friend of mine, a former missionary to North Thailand, Viggo Sogaard. At that time he was a graduate student in communications studying under James Engel of Wheaton Graduate School. Engel is well known as a specialist in marketing research; hence, certain insights from marketing analysis stimulated Sogaard in the development of the model which is now known as the "Engel scale." It has been revised and modified by Engel and other missiologists. (See Figure 5.)

The Engel scale depicts the spiritual-decision process and uses the countdown methodology to show the period of awareness, period of decision, and the period of incorporation similar to Tippett's model. Engel affirms that the Great Commission is not fulfilled simply by proclaiming the Gospel. Rather, the new believer needs to be baptized and taught to observe all that Christ has commanded the Church. Becoming a disciple is thus regarded as a process which continues over a life span as believers are conformed to the image of Christ (Philippians 1:6).

> It appears, then, that the Great Commission contains three related but distinctly different communication mandates: (1) to proclaim the message; (2) to persuade the unbeliever; and (3) to cultivate the believer. Part of the problem with the harvest comes from fuzzy thinking at precisely this point because of a tendency to blur the essential distinctions between these communication functions (Engel & Norton 1977:44).

The usefulness of the Engel countdown scale is that it clearly shows how the process of making a decision for Christ actually operates. People who know little of the Good News are included on the scale along with those who believe and then press on to growth and maturity in Christ. It is true that some decisions may not be quite as lineal as the Engel scale suggests. Surely it is possible for several stages to be going on at the same time. Information gathering and decision-making may be simultaneous in some instances. Also, the time factor enters in. For some engrossed in the process of conversion many months or years may be required. Information may be supplied spasmodically. Others may come to a decision more rapidly with a minimum of prior information.

Other variables may be present in the conversion process which are not included in the Engel scale. While the Engel scale may apply to most cultures, it may not be significant for all cultures. For some people there are many little

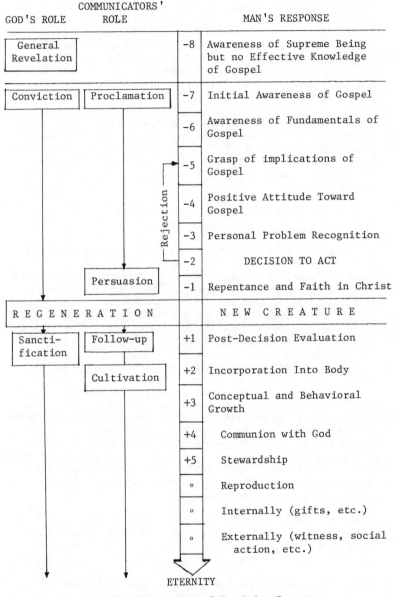

Figure 5. The Spiritual-Decision Process
(Engel & Norton 1975:45)

decisions which take place before the major ones. It is impossible for a scale of this nature to include everything; nevertheless, it is a useful device to enable us to look more objectively at the spiritual-decision process. The missionary will be helped to realize that his ministry may be at any one stage in the process, or it may consist of caring for young believers at several stages in their Christian growth and development.

Conversion to Christ is an important process which leads to culture change. As conversion takes place in cross-cultural settings the degree of culture change will vary. Hence, it is mandatory that the missionary understand the process of innovation and how the agent of change relates to the receptor people.

THE IMPORTANCE OF CONTEXTUALIZATION OF THE CHRISTIAN MESSAGE

Since the introduction of the Christian message inevitably contributes to innovation and culture change, missionaries should be alert to the importance of contextualization of the Christian message. After understanding what contextualization means, the missionary should be aware of dynamic equivalence translations and the dynamic equivalence church.

What is Contextualization?

The term "contextualization" refers to the sustained effort to present the Christian message in such a way that it becomes a part of the cultural context of the receptor people. It has to do with communication and may be considered the basic issue of cross-cultural communication. "Our real objective . . . is not a change of content . . , but rather a fitting of the same content into such culturally meaningful forms as will be fit vehicles for the communication of the message" (Nida 1960:180). This will require real work and a good understanding of cultural backgrounds in order to put it into practice.

The Christian message must be planted within the cultural milieu of a particular people. The Gospel is powerful and capable of instigating cultural change. Knowledge of the cultural system in which the missionary works is an essential.

> For the reformer who chooses to work within
> the system it means that one of the primary
> tasks is to know the institution to be changed

better than the ones who now control it and
know it. Here again it is obvious that the
person who does his homework most thoroughly
has a tremendous advantage over everyone else
(Schaller 1972:46).

While the Christian message will undoubtedly cause some
culture change, it need not and should not destroy the culture of the people who have accepted the Gospel. It must
become a part of the cultural system and this must be done
without completely rebuilding the system. Keesing comments,

An important dimension of the acculturation
process is congruence between the two cultural
systems involved . . . if two ideational systems
share certain common premises and values, or can
be fitted together, a creative synthesis between
them may be possible that otherwise would not.
The rapid success of missionaries in some areas
and decades of failure in others must reflect not
the diligence and zeal of the salesman, but the
salability of their product. Whether Christian
belief can be fitted into a people's conceptual
world without completely rebuilding it is clearly
a crucial variable (1971:354-355).

It is true that the salability of the product may be a
serious problem with some groups, but the ways in which the
salesmen operate will be vital concerns in the work of Christian missions. Understanding the cultural context and attempting to plant the Christian message within it without destroy-
ing the people or their culture will continue to be the challenge of contextualization. Missionaries will need to depend
on the wisdom of the Holy Spirit when making applications in
this crucial area.

Dynamic Equivalence Translations

Another aspect of contextualization and an important key
in the process is the dynamic equivalence model. All communication consists of forms and meanings. "God's desire to convey his message to humans within the human cultural and linguistic frame of reference necessitates the translation of
God's casebook" (Kraft 1979:262).

The mention of "frame of reference" by Kraft is to be
understood as everything which makes up the cultural context
of a particular group of people. Their worldview, including

the social, religious, and linguistic heritage, would all be in a group's frame of reference. For instance, Iran and Jordan would represent a frame of reference which is strongly dominated by Islamic thought. This would be an important consideration in planning a missionary strategy in these countries.

Kraft's mention of "God's casebook" refers to the Bible. Since the Bible is filled with case studies, illustrations, and models for the Christian worker, he likens it to God's casebook. The Bible has always been and is a foundation stone for the work of Christian missions.

Bible translation has always been a vital aspect of the missionary task. "When working with Scripture, a literal translation of the form (formal correspondence) may conceal or distort the true meaning" (Engel 1979:272). A literal translation is one in which the translators attempt a word for word literal equivalence as they translate. This can be a very difficult task. In some instances one word in Hebrew or Greek can only be expressed by using several words in English. There may be a breadth of meaning in the source language which cannot fully be translated into English.

It needs to be kept in mind that meanings of words in the receptor language change over a period of years; hence, the translation may need to be up-dated in order to communicate the actual meaning clearly. An example would be the King James rendering of Philippians 4:6, "Be careful for nothing . . . ." which has a confused meaning for the contemporary English reader. It actually distorts the real meaning. In the 1600's when the King James Version was published, "Be careful for nothing" referred to being worried or anxious, but in contemporary English usage it means no such thing.

In the New International Version of Philippians 4:6 we read, "Do not be anxious about anything, but in everything by prayer and petition, with thanksgiving, present your requests to God." In the Living Bible the rendering is even more vibrant with meaning: "Don't worry about anything; instead pray about everything. . . ." The essence of the dynamic equivalence approach is that the form is changed to preserve the meaning. Engel affirms this approach as he writes, "By the way, Scripture translators who have had any degree of acceptance in the church have always followed the dynamic equivalence approach" (1979:272). This helps to explain the great popularity and usefulness of the Living Bible in the contemporary English-speaking world.

Perhaps a word of caution regarding the Living Bible is in order. When it comes to translation of the Bible there is always a need to remain accurate. Some biblical scholars feel that the Living Bible is not a good example of accuracy in meaning. For this reason some prefer to call the Living Bible a paraphrase instead of a translation because the translator has taken some liberties in expressing the meaning of the text. One of the chief strengths of the Living Bible is its feeling communication. Contemporary English readers feel that the Word of God is being communicated to them in a clear and lucid manner. Nevertheless, forms have their own meanings and should be translated as accurately as possible. Translators ought not to take liberties in translating forms. Accuracy is required.

Kraft refers to Phillips' "essential principles of translation" which guided him in producing a hearer-oriented translation:

> The task of the translator as Phillips (and more recent translation theorists) sees it is to 'incarnate' the written word in the language of the receptors. It should (1) sound natural to them, and (2) have an impact upon them as equivalent as possible to that experienced by the original readers of the original writings in the original languages. This process of necessity involves translators in interpretation (1979:263).

This type of translation will be most effective in communicating the Christian message in an understandable and meaningful manner.

Dynamic Equivalence Churches

The theory of dynamic equivalence also applies to the formation of the Christian church wherever it may be planted. The concept implies that a dynamic equivalence church would produce the same type of impact in the present context as the early church produced in the first century. A dynamically equivalent church may be defined as one which:

> (1) conveys to its members truly Christian meanings, (2) functions within its own society in the name of Christ, meeting the felt needs of that society and producing within it the same Christian impact as the first-century church in its day, and (3) is couched in cultural forms that are as nearly indigenous as possible (Kraft 1979:49).

In order to accomplish such a task it will be necessary to avoid forms and practices exported from another culture, unless, of course, these forms or practices are desired and willingly accepted by the host society of their own will and volition. If so, the normal channels of culture change would be in operation. "A contemporary church, like a contemporary translation, should impress the uninitiated observer as an original production in the contemporary culture, not as a badly fitted import from somewhere else" (Kraft 1979:318).

It will not necessarily be an easy task to establish dynamic equivalence churches; nevertheless, the challenge is a worthy one and should be the missionary's goal.

It should be recognized that dynamic equivalence often is hard to achieve. The New Testament is not definitive when it comes to form and practice in the church. In fact, it only provides glimpses of first-century contextualization (Engel 1979:273).

The dynamics of culture change have many implications for the Christian missionary. Tradition and change are ever with us. Innovation as a process needs to be understood. It will aid the missionary task. Because the missionary is an agent of change he will need to see his role carefully in stimulating culture change. Conversion and contextualization are likewise important aspects which are linked to culture change within the missionary enterprise. Thus, there is a need for the missionary to be prepared well so that he will understand the dynamics of culture change which is definitely involved in missionary endeavor. Church planting in a cross-cultural context involves the missionary in the dynamics of culture change; hence, this subject is worthy of consideration.

8

Preparing Bicultural Missionaries

Living today in a world which has become a global village we come in contact with people representing a variety of different cultures. In order to communicate the Gospel in cross-cultural settings it is necessary to develop a bicultural perspective. The capacity to understand and accept the cultural ways of other groups of people, while at the same time recognizing the validity of one's own cultural heritage, may be called a bicultural perspective. Factors which will help one to become a bicultural person are the following: contrasting monoculturalism versus biculturalism, becoming a "world Christian," involvement in summer missions, gaining cross-cultural experience, and aiming toward the planting of "dynamic equivalence churches."

MONOCULTURALISM VERSUS BICULTURALISM

Many North Americans have grown up in a monocultural world. Yet, all around us we live in a multi-cultural mosaic of ethnic diversity. Nevertheless, it is easy to take for granted that our own life-ways are the best. Some simply refuse to work with differences they encounter among other peoples. Others even ignore or look down upon those who speak a different dialect of English. Frequently such people have learned to use ridicule and even mockery to show a speaker with an accent that he is an alien, an outsider, and consequently rejected. Instead of practicing acceptance and mutual respect we sometimes drive a wedge between ourselves and the people we desire to influence for Christ. A monocultural approach is selfish and harmful to a good climate

143

for communication; however, a bicultural approach facilitates communication.

> The monocultural approach to the behavior of others is to see in what ways that behavior is understandable to the one viewing it and how it can be changed to conform to the expectations of the one viewing it. The cross-cultural or bicultural approach lets man be man and God be God in evaluating behavior. . . Such an approach results in maximum responsibility of the person and allows him to have those sociocultural uniquenesses that reinforce his identity and encourage mature growth in the Christian faith. Spiritual conflict is thus not intensified because of unnecessary social conflict (Mayers 1974:242).

Missionaries must learn the bicultural approach if they wish to communicate effectively. To practice monoculturalism as an approach to Christian ministry in a cross-cultural context is to close the door--at least in part--for further communication.

Adapting to Other Cultures

Flexibility and adaptability are qualities every missionary must develop. Entering a new cultural milieu demands that the newcomer make an effort to adapt to the conventional life-ways of the host country. Difference and variety will be immediately apparent. A strange climate, new foods, simple modes of transportation, and different-looking people all combine to challenge the missionary's capacity to adapt.

A missionary who has learned to accept himself as a person is generally more able to accept others who are different as valid persons. Mutual respect should follow as the missionary grows in love and appreciation for the people of the host society. This, of course, will take time; nevertheless, a positive approach to people is most beneficial in establishing rapport. Accepting people should lead to an appreciation of their cultural ways as well. Hiebert describes the process:

> Something happens to us when we adapt to a new culture. We become bicultural people. Our parochialism, based on our unquestioned feeling that there is really only one way to live, and our way is it, is shattered. We must deal with cultural variety, with the fact that people build cultures

in different ways, and that they believe their
cultures are better than ours. Aside from some
curiosity at our foreignness, they are not interested in learning our ways (Glasser et. al. 1976:51).

It is true that in the process of adapting and becoming
bicultural the missionary may become alienated from family
members and friends in the homeland. They find it difficult
to understand that the missionary appreciates and loves the
people and their strange life-ways. The missionary simply
looks at things differently. He is in the process of becoming
a bicultural person. Hiebert suggests, "We have moved from a
philosophy that assumes uniformity to one that has had to cope
with variety, and our old friends often don't understand us.
In time we may find our closest associates among other bicultural people" (Glasser et. al. 1976:51).

Checking Cultural Baggage

Traditionally missionaries have maintained strong theological orientations. The Bible contained the truth, and the
missionary learned biblical truth in Bible colleges and seminaries. Having been sent out by local churches to minister
the Gospel among non-Christians worldwide (commonly called
"the heathen"), they trusted that the Holy Spirit would apply
the truth to the hearts of non-Christians and they would be
converted. "An unfortunate side effect of such an approach
was the communication of much of the missionaries' culture
with the truth. The new convert not only accepted Christ but
much of the missionaries' life-ways as well" (Mayers 1974:
26-27). This unfortunate development is referred to as cultural baggage.

Many national believers gained the impression that they
had to become like the white man in order to be Christians.
This concept was not necessarily taught by the missionaries
explicitly; nevertheless, it was somehow communicated in many
areas of the world. Becoming a bicultural missionary helps
to avoid this hindrance.

The exciting aspect of today's learning
explosion is that any person can be trained to
face the challenges of change quite naturally and
without anxiety. This training derives from the
behavioral sciences which, when teamed up with
sound theology, can help the missionary introduce
the Gospel of Jesus Christ without its being encum-
bered with the cultural baggage of the sending

society. The missionary at ease within the
change setting can be sure that the message he
is communicating is truly the message of salvation in Jesus Christ (Mayers 1974:19).

The bicultural approach seeks to temper the staid and
stern theological approach by helping the missionary to be
aware of other peoples as valid persons within their own cultural systems. It attempts to make a distinction between the
Gospel and the culture in order to avoid the extremes of
ethnocentrism and the exporting of cultural baggage abroad.

Effective Ministry

The bicultural missionary is one who has learned to accept
himself and others who may be vastly different from himself.
He is able to develop mutual respect and to express love and
appreciation for national brethren. He will recognize social
groupings and readily identify different groups and sub-groups
in the course of his missionary work. Recognizing the validity of distinct societies he will make every effort to understand the cultural system before attempting to function as an
agent of change. As the missionary discovers and understands
the cultural system of a people, effective means of communication with its members will begin to emerge. The Holy Spirit
will guide the bicultural missionary in the development of
effective strategies for sharing the Good News and in stimulating church growth.

The bicultural missionary is able to be at home in two
or more cultures without undue stress or anxiety. He will
expect a measure of culture shock and understand his reactions
to it while cultural adjustment is taking place. He will
seek to communicate the Good News of Jesus Christ in a culturally acceptable and relevant way, and the Holy Spirit will
guide in just how that approach should be developed. The
prospects of positive results will be greater and the bicultural servant of the Lord will have greater peace and joy in
serving Jesus Christ in a cross-cultural setting.

A truly bicultural individual can introduce
the Gospel in any culture or subculture without
the accompanying cultural baggage that is potential for enslavement of the person and falsifica-
tion of precept or truth. His range of variation
of life-style or norm is increased, so he is comfortable and at peace with peoples of diverse
styles or norms, while at the same time he is

protected from abandonment of his own principles
(Mayers 1974:243).

BECOMING A WORLD CHRISTIAN

As a believer grows in Christian maturity there should
follow a growing awareness of the world's spiritual needs.
It is easy to become selfish, thinking in terms of personal
salvation through faith in Jesus Christ as a mere ticket to
heaven. Such thinking is unworthy of a mature follower of
Christ. The challenge to become a world Christian is a
stimulating motivation toward Christian growth.

Every Christian is Not a Missionary!

Considerable confusion has been created by sincere evangelists and Bible teachers who have proclaimed that every
Christian is a missionary. Taken at face value the statement is misleading. Such an appeal has likely challenged
some complacent Christians to consider a missionary vocation;
however, others have become severely guilt-ridden. C. Peter
Wagner considers the statement as "theological humbug." He
feels that this statement has stimulated two other kinds of
reactions that have not helped the missionary cause:

1. Some well-meaning Christians have actually
   gone to the mission field and washed out because they really were not missionaries to
   start with.
2. Some Christians have not gone to the mission
   field, but as a result of taking this appeal
   seriously, they have for many years found
   themselves plagued by serious and unnecessary
   guilt feelings, thereby losing part of their
   Christian joy (1974:29).

Those who make the statement, "Every Christian is a missionary," likely mean that every Christian is a witness. On
the basis of Acts 1:8 this statement is theologically sound.
We should also note here that a person can be either a good
witness or a poor witness. One who aspires to be a world
Christian should purpose to become a good and faithful witness for Jesus Christ.

What is a World Christian?

God is concerned for the peoples of the world. This is
why He sent His beloved Son, as John wrote, "For God so loved

the world that he gave his one and only Son, that whoever believes in him shall not perish but have everlasting life"
(3:16 NIV). Since God was so concerned for sinful mankind,
how much more ought we who claim the name of Christ to be concerned for the salvation of lost men and women around the
world. While it is true that every Christian is not a missionary, every believer ought to be a world Christian.

A world Christian is one who believes in Great Commission
missions and is willing to become involved in whatever way
possible to achieve God's will "to make disciples of all the
nations" (Matthew 28:19 NIV). This does not mean that every
Christian will be able to make disciples of every nation, but
every Christian should have God's concern close to his/her
heart. Such a Christian will want to work with every ounce
of energy to see God's will accomplished.

A world Christian will take time to acquaint himself with
the biblical bases for missions as recorded in the Old and
New Testaments. Having studied the Word of God, the conviction
of world evangelization will be confirmed as a matter of contemporary Christian concern. Not all Christians will express
their concern in the same ways. Nevertheless, God's will in
this matter will be carefully discerned and obedience will
follow. "A world Christian is one who sees the mystery of God
unfolded for all the nations of the world to see and accept--
people who see God's concern now for the nations in this end
time" (Graham 1975:5). Such a Christian will be one in agreement with the Apostle Paul when he wrote,

> Now to him who is able to establish you by
> my gospel and the proclamation of Jesus Christ,
> according to the revelation of the mystery hidden
> for long ages past, but now revealed and made
> known through the prophetic writings by the command
> of the eternal God, so that all nations might be-
> lieve and obey him (Romans 16:25,26 NIV).

Categories of World Christians

In his very helpful pamphlet entitled, "Everything You
Need to Know to Become a World Christian" (1975), published
by the Fellowship of World Christians, D. Bruce Graham de-
scribes three types of world Christians first outlined by
Ralph Winter. These may be found in most local congregations.
He calls them beavers, eagles, and mallards.

The beaver category of world Christian is the one who is

heavily involved in the local church but has world awareness.
He has seen God's highest priority of reaching the unreached,
but his present concern concentrates on the local task at
home. Like the beaver, he works diligently yet remains close
to one location. Many such beavers are the backbone of the
local churches all around the world.

The second category of world Christians, called eagles,
refers to the Christian who has some kind of special indirect
involvement in the task of world evangelization. He may leave
many tasks to the beavers in the local setting. Yet, as he
soars further afield he sees the broader picture of God's missionary task. Such a person may not become involved overseas
or in a cross-cultural setting; however he may host a mission
board prayer meeting in his home. He will keep abreast of
what God is doing in a particular sphere of labor whether it
is in Asia, Africa, Europe, or Latin America. He may serve
as an advisory member for a mission board.

The third category of world Christian to which Graham refers is the mallard duck. The mallard Christian is one who
actually becomes a missionary in a cross-cultural setting.
Because of the great ethnic diversity in many parts of the
world, the mallard world Christian does not necessarily have
to leave his homeland to engage in cross-cultural ministry.
It may take place at home or abroad as God may lead. Just
as the mallard migrates to remote areas, so the cross-cultural missionary may be led of God across cultural barriers
to proclaim the Gospel. Graham emphasizes a helpful distinction as he writes,

> Notice that all the differences between
> these animals are not the result of more effort
> or spirituality on the part of one, but rather
> that each of these animals has been equipped by
> the Creator and is uniquely suited to and happiest
> when carrying out his complementary part of the
> task (1975:2).

It is clear from these analogies that God needs beavers,
eagles, and mallards in order to accomplish His task of
world evangelization. The evangelical churches today need
this challenging and practical emphasis. World Christians
are in great demand in God's missionary enterprise. Presenting the challenge and excitement of contemporary missions,
David Bryant has written *In the Gap* (1979), published by
Inter-Varsity Press. He refers to world Christians as those
who have taken a stand that says:

We want to accept personal responsibility
for reaching some of the earth's unreached,
especially from among the billions at the widest
end of the Gap who can only be reached through
major new efforts by God's people. Among every
people-group where there is no vital, evangelizing
Christian community there should be one, there
must be one, there shall be one. Together we want
to help make this happen (1979:72).

How to Become a World Christian

In becoming a world Christian there are at least five
steps you may take. First, make a decision before God that
you want to become a world Christian. This decision may mean
sacrificing worldly ambitions in order to do the will of God.
Paul challenged the Roman Christians to be living sacrifices:

Therefore, I urge you, brothers, in view of
God's mercy, to offer yourselves as living sacrifices holy and pleasing to God--which is your
spiritual worship. Do not conform any longer to
the pattern of this world, but be transformed by
the renewing of your mind. Then you will be able
to test and approve what God's will is--his good,
pleasing and perfect will (Romans 12:1-2 NIV).

Secondly, link yourself with a missionary-minded church.
If you desire to grow in your missionary commitment, you will
need the fellowship of other like-minded believers. A faithful pastor who preaches and teaches from the great missionary
texts of the Scriptures will be used of God to deepen your
capacity as a world Christian. The local church should be
the seed-bed for a great harvest of world Christians.

Thirdly, study for yourself the biblical basis for missions. Both the Old and New Testaments contain teaching on
the theme of missions. The life of our Lord Jesus Christ
was centered in doing His Father's will. Thus, He could say
to His disciples, "As the Father has sent me, so send I you"
(John 20:21). Study the book of Acts, and especially the
life and ministry of the Apostle Paul. The dynamic of missionary outreach to others dominates this particular New
Testament book.

Fourthly, keep yourself aware of what God is doing in
missions. Attend missionary meetings and talk with missionaries personally. Subscribe to missionary magazines and

read up on what is actually being done in various parts of
the world. Read missionary biographies. They become stimulating examples of how God uses His servants in missionary
service. Try to attend missionary conferences where the Word
of God is taught, and where God's servants share reports of
their ministry.

Fifthly, begin to pray for missionaries by name regularly.
Write to them and keep abreast of their work and their personal
needs. Develop a prayer list of missionaries and works of God
for which you pray consistently. Your Christian life will be
challenged to grow and expand as you pray.

These are only a few ways in which to become a world Christian. They do not just happen automatically. As you take the
first step, the Holy Spirit begins to work in your life, di-
recting your path step by step. Begin to grow as a world
Christian and God will broaden your vision and expand your
horizons to see vast multitudes who as yet do not know our
Lord Jesus Christ. About 87 per cent of the world's population can only be reached by cross-cultural proclamation of
the Gospel. Many thousands of world Christians--beavers,
eagles, and mallards--are needed to accomplish the unfinished
task.

LEARNING THROUGH SUMMER OR SHORT TERM MISSIONS

The contemporary missionary movement contains an inner
force which makes it one of the most dynamic enterprises of
the twentieth century. During the past two decades Christian
young people have become concerned to assist in the missionary
cause. Numbering only a few hundred in the early 1960's, by
1974 they numbered over 4,000 as they became involved in
summer and short term missions (Kane 1974:384). By 1980 they
numbered over 17,000! Through summer and short term missions
young people gain missionary awareness, plus actual involvement in various aspects of the missionary endeavor.

Gaining an Awareness of Missions

As young people volunteer to serve at home and abroad in
short term ministries the Holy Spirit stimulates within them
a growing awareness of what God is doing. They have opportunities to meet experienced career missionaries. Also, they
witness firsthand what missionary work is all about. They
become involved in simple but helpful tasks that further the
missionary cause.

Some teams of young people become involved in work projects such as building a chapel, a clinic, or a dormitory building. On Sundays they worship with the local Christians and may be involved in tract distribution, visitation, or music ministries with national Christians. This type of involvement creates a growing sense of awareness of the spiritual needs of others. Other young people serve in direct evangelistic ministries, musical groups, drama, and visitation.

Since the needs of each land are different, the types of ministry will vary from country to country. Language barriers may well limit the scope of their ministry. Nevertheless, these young people seek to work with existing evangelical missions and under the direction of the local missionaries or national church leaders. They raise their own support through home churches, family, and friends; hence, they are not a financial burden to the cooperating missionaries. Some young people even contribute sums of money to the work projects in which they participate, and then supply free labor to complete the job.

Summer Involvement

It has become popular in recent years for Christian young people to involve themselves in summer missions. The length of involvement may vary from six to twelve weeks during their school vacation period. Modern day transportation facilitates this noble effort. Becoming involved is a challenge to spiritual growth as well as to personal development and maturity as persons. These are worthy factors to consider. Young people learn to trust God to supply their needs. They learn to trust Him in adjusting to living and working in a strange environment. They also learn to trust God in the area of personal relationships. Though limited, this cross-cultural involvement is very helpful in creating a bicultural attitude which is so necessary for missionary endeavor.

Many mission boards have greatly benefited from summer missions. At first they were slow to respond, thinking that missionary work demands career involvement. While it is true that long term missionary service is most beneficial to church planting and in developing national leadership, there are many tasks that summer workers can do. Young people today want to get involved. They want to learn by doing. The practical work projects which young people can do makes it possible for missionaries to do other tasks. At the same time, God the Holy Spirit is opening the eyes of these young people to the mission fields of the world.

Short Term Involvement

Summer missions is not the only type of involvement. Many denominational missions have encouraged young people to consider short term commitments which may involve a length of service from six months to three years in duration. Often these short term opportunities exist in conjunction with institutions, such as schools, hospitals and clinics. Thus, teachers and medical personnel are in demand, and they perform a notable service to the missions and churches they serve in various parts of the world.

Short term missionaries may relieve career missionaries for holidays, study leaves, or furloughs. Such help is much appreciated by the cooperating missions. The short termer also gains a firsthand knowledge concerning missionary work. God often uses this practical experience to guide an individual's life. Many short termers have later become full time missionaries because of the short term experience they had earlier. Such experiences help to create awareness of spiritual needs. They also help the participants to realize the importance of a bicultural approach to missionary endeavor.

Evaluating Short Term Missions

Among young people today short term missions are popular. Among some older mission board personnel there are doubts, criticisms, and suspicions regarding short term missions. The younger generation is mobile and transportation is fast and reasonable in cost. Young people want to be where the action is. Fifty years ago such an approach to missionary involvement was impossible. Today it is a reality and the trend would indicate even greater involvement in the years ahead.

There are both advantages and disadvantages connected with short term and summer missions. Among the advantages J. Herbert Kane notes the following: short term programs appeal to youth today; they help solve the manpower problem on the fields; they may lead to a life-time of service; they free career missionaries for other duties; and they bring a reflex blessing to the home churches (1974:375-377). In some denominations more than 50 per cent of their present career missionaries began as short termers. The results of some preliminary studies on the effectiveness of short term missions for missionary recruitment are summarized by Kane:

> The short term abroad program is still comparatively young, and reliable statistics are

difficult to obtain. To further complicate the
matter, the situation differs from mission to
mission, but it is generally believed that 20%
of the short termers become career missionaries
after one term abroad. Of those who spend two
or more short terms abroad, 50% sign up for life,
which means that in the long run short terms
abroad is a good thing for the cause of missions
(1974:376).

Short term missions spark enthusiasm and idealism among
young people. Many have grown tremendously in their awareness of spiritual needs in other lands. When they returned
to their home churches and shared their reports of involvement, others were stirred and blessed. Thus, the cause of
missions is stimulated in local churches. Young people who
were students in Bible institutes and colleges returned to
their campuses with zeal and enthusiasm which soon spread
among their classmates. Many mission boards have reported
that former short term workers have joined their missions on
a long term basis and are presently in active service.

There are problems connected with short term missions as
well. The area of communication is a big one. In many countries abroad English is spoken little or not at all; hence,
short termers are frustrated when it comes to verbal communication. Their lack of experience is another factor. As
young people they cannot be expected to have vast experience
in the Lord's work, and so their contribution to the work may
be quite limited.

The problem of acculturation must be faced. It takes time
for people to learn to live and relate in a new culture. A
few weeks or a few months on the field is not enough time to
make a good adjustment to the culture and people. The high
cost of summer missions, especially, has been a concern to
some. Is it really worth it? Some have voiced real doubt at
this point. Then, too, the whole area of lack of continuity
must be faced realistically. Who will carry on when the short
termer departs for home? These are problem areas which have
emerged, and they must be considered carefully.

While there are both pluses and minuses related to short
term missions, young people today tend to favor the plus side.
Many mission boards are seeing the hand of God in this contemporary trend. It may not be the complete answer to the
problem of missionary recruitment, but short term missions
have made and are making a positive contribution. The cross-

cultural experience gained by the young people enables them to see the need for a bicultural approach to missions. This, too, is a positive factor which must not be overlooked.

OTHER TYPES OF CROSS-CULTURAL EXPOSURE

In order to obtain a bicultural perspective it is helpful to gain a measure of cross-cultural exposure. There are many ways this can be accomplished. Among them are the Peace Corps, military service, government service, short term missions, and identifying with other ethnic groups.

Peace Corps

The Peace Corps, established during the John F. Kennedy presidency, has enabled hundreds of young people to travel and work in other countries. The training program for the Peace Corps is well done and serves to prepare the worker for cross-cultural contact. Following assignment to an overseas post the Peace Corps worker must learn the language and begin to communicate with the people. Everything is new—food, friends, flowers, and forms! Gradually the Peace Corps worker learns the cultural ways of the people. Within two years identification with the people has been greatly intensified. But, it is now time to return home. Some Peace Corps workers have extended their tour of duty in order to make a further contribution to their host countries.

The Peace Corps provided a great opportunity for cross-cultural exposure. In the process these workers developed bicultural attitudes. Some became Christians while overseas, and a few have returned as missionaries to the countries where they served as Peace Corps workers.

Military Service

War is never pleasant. Yet, because of war and compulsory military service thousands of young men have been sent overseas to serve their country. They experienced culture shock. They complained about the food, the loneliness, the heat and the filth of their duty stations. Some G.I.'s came to know Christ while overseas; others were Christians before they entered the service. I was among the latter, and God used my army experience in Tokyo to open my eyes to the spiritual needs of millions of Japanese. The cross-cultural exposure was a valuable asset in preparing me to be a bicultural person. Instead of returning to Japan, God led me and my wife to Thailand for twelve years of missionary service.

World War II was used of God to challenge numerous young
men to consider the mission fields of the Philippines and
Japan. The Far Eastern Gospel Crusade was founded by a group
of Christian ex-servicemen who had a burden to proclaim the
Gospel in the Far East. Thus, their cross-cultural exposure
resulted in the birth of a new mission board which now numbers several hundred missionaries.

Government Service

Civil service jobs abroad for the government have provided excellent cross-cultural exposure. A new awareness of
people and their needs quickly becomes apparent to the government worker in a strange land. For the Christian serving
overseas there is the added dimension of spiritual concern for
others outside of Christ. The Holy Spirit works in strange
ways in calling out those who should be serving God instead of
"Uncle Sam." The experience overseas has been invaluable
throughout history. God has used cross-cultural government
service to prepare bicultural workers for missionary endeavor.

Identifying with Other Ethnic Groups

The cultures of the United States and Canada are like a
huge mosaic composed of beautiful people from many parts of
the world. Christians should take time to meet and become
acquainted with people from other ethnic backgrounds. We have
all been created in the image of God; thus, there is no reason
why we should not appreciate one another. Our tendency is to
have associations with those who are like we are while ignoring or rejecting others who may be different. A summer missions project in a Black or Hispanic ghetto of a major city
would be an excellent challenge for Christian service, plus
an opportunity to gain a bicultural perspective. Other ethnic groups are all around us and all of them need the Gospel.
The challenge to witness for Christ is ever before us; obedience to the Lord is sometimes lacking.

These and other ways of gaining cross-cultural exposure
are stepping stones toward becoming a bicultural person. God
is able to use such experiences to create that bicultural perspective in His servants which is so necessary for effective
cross-cultural ministry.

AIMING TOWARD THE PLANTING OF DYNAMIC EQUIVALENCE CHURCHES

Historically, ever since the first century A.D., the work
of missions has resulted in the establishment of local churches.

This development has followed the command of our Lord who said, ". . . I will build my church, and the gates of Hades will not overcome it" (Matthew 16:18 NIV). In further developing our bicultural perspective it will be helpful to note four vital factors; namely, the necessity for evangelism, the importance of the church, and the contrast between formal equivalence churches and dynamic equivalence churches.

The Necessity for Evangelism

In order for churches to exist there must first be evangelism. During the International Congress on World Evangelization at Lausanne, Switzerland, in 1974, Ralph Winter alerted the delegates to the fact that all evangelistic tasks are not alike. Winter noted that there are important differences between monoculturalism and cross-cultural evangelism. Many non-Christians can be evangelized by their culturally near neighbors who speak the same language and have the same customs.

> A technical term for such monocultural evangelism is evangelism one or E-1. However, many non-Christians cannot be reached by E-1 evangelism because there is not yet any viable witnessing Christian group made up of persons of their own culture. In order for them to be reached they obviously need missionaries who are willing to cross cultural boundaries, learn their language and customs, and present the Gospel in terms that can be clearly understood. A technical term for this cross-cultural evangelism is evangelism two (E-1) or, if the cultural boundary happens to be a more formidable one, evangelism three (E-3) (Wagner & Dayton 1981:20).

It may be helpful to clarify the E-1, E-2 and E-3 terminology. E-1 refers to evangelism among near neighbors--same language, same customs, same culture. E-2 refers to evangelism among peoples who are sufficiently different to make the founding of separate congregations desirable to act as a base for effective outreach to others in that same culture. Los Angeles Blacks or Cree Indians of northern Canada may be considered examples of E-2 type evangelism. E-3 refers to evangelism among peoples who are totally different. They are the culturally distant ones where it is mandatory to learn a completely new language and a new system of cultural ways. The U.S. Center for World Mission (Pasadena, CA) believes "that a full 80% of the world's non-Christians will initially

require E-2/3 evangelism if they are going to become Christians" (Wagner & Dayton 1981:20).

Since the bulk of the missionary task must take place in
the categories of E-2/3 evangelism, strategies must be developed to accomplish the unfinished task. This challenge has
led the Lausanne Committee for World Evangelization to advocate
the people-group approach to world evangelization. A helpful
idea in the people-approach to world evangelization was found
in the theory of the diffusion of innovation and information.

> New ideas flow along the lines of natural
> human relationships. Ideas spread most rapidly
> within a close-knit group and are often blocked
> when they reach the boundaries of that group.
> An analysis of the spread of the gospel during
> and since New Testament times verifies this dimen-
> sion of human life. Attempting to discover God's
> unique strategy for confronting a specific people
> group with the Gospel is not only a comprehendible
> and believeable approach, but it focuses resources
> in the most effective way humanly possible. Once
> the gospel impregnates a people group, and a viable
> church is brought into being by the Holy Spirit,
> that church is an intimate part of its context and
> has within it the capability to evangelize the rest
> of the people group (Wagner & Dayton 1981:25).

As a strategy for effective evangelism and church planting
the people-group approach has great potential. It is both
biblical and practical.[1]

The Importance of the Church

Following the ascension of Christ (Acts 1) and the descent
of the Holy Spirit (Acts 2) the establishment of the church
began in earnest. As the early apostles proclaimed the Good
News concerning the cross and the resurrection, many believed
and became followers of Jesus Christ. At first a majority of
them were Jewish Christians. The ministry of the Apostle Paul

---

[1]For detailed information concerning the people-group
approach to world evangelization, consult *Unreached Peoples
'81* by C. Peter Wagner and Edward R. Dayton (Elgin, IL: David
C. Cook, 1981), and *That Everyone May Hear* by Edward R. Dayton
(Monrovia, CA: MARC 1980).

during his missionary journeys resulted in the formation of
many churches in Asia Minor and southern Europe. Church history records the struggles and victories of the church from
the first century to the present time. The spread of the
church of Jesus Christ has always been an important aspect of
the dynamic Christian movement. That work continues today on
all continents and is carried on by Christians of all races
and nationalities. The form which the church has taken has
varied from culture to culture and from nation to nation.
Nevertheless, church planting and church growth must be priorities for missionary endeavor. Every effort must be made
to evangelize people-groups in order that churches may be
established in every group. This is a gigantic task, but it
brings much glory to our God.

Formal Equivalence Churches

One form the church has taken has been to copy the exact
form of the foreign church which founded it. This approach
has been called the formal-correspondence church. This type
of church is often rather slavish in following the structure
and polity of the parent church. Concerning this approach
Charles Kraft comments:

> It will always smack of foreignness, of in-
> sensitivity to the surrounding culture, of inappro-
> priateness to the real needs of the people and the
> real message of God to them. Its forms have not
> been exchanged, via transculturation, for those
> appropriate in the new setting (1979:319).

Although establishing indigenous churches has long been a
goal of contemporary missions, often in practice, even though
churches have been formed with national pastors, national
finances, and national leaders, the churches are often more or
less carbon copies of their Euro-American counterparts. In a
true sense this type of church is not really indigenous, although outwardly it may give that appearance.

Dynamic Equivalence Churches

As the church emerges in any culture it should feel at
home there and be an integral part of that cultural milieu.
Nationals then feel it is their church and not the foreigner's
church. This means that architecture, leadership, and forms
of worship reflect the cultural values of a particular society.

Contemporary churches should bear the same
resemblance to the scriptural models (both Old
Testament and New Testament) of God's interaction
with humans in culture that a faithful dynamic-
equivalence translation of the Scriptures bears
to his interaction with humans in language (Kraft
1979:318).

The dynamic of the Christian message will be the same, but
the form the church takes will vary from culture to culture.
This development will not be the same as carbon copy formal
equivalence churches. The potential for growth and development will be far greater if this approach is used.

Outside observers who are not Christians should be impressed with the church as an original production within the
cultural setting and not as a strange import from outside.
Since the original proclaimers of the Gospel in many cultures
were foreigners from the West, this approach is not the easi-
est to accomplish. Yet, this type of a church will make the
greater impact within a given culture in contrast to the formal correspondence church. Aspects of foreignness and outside domination are thereby avoided. As Kraft explains,

A dynamic-equivalence church produces an impact on the people of the society of which it is
a part equivalent to that which the scripturally
described peoples of God produced upon the original hearers. In that equivalence the church will
need leadership, organization, education, worship,
buildings, behavioral standards, and means of expressing Christian love and concern to the people
of its own culture who have not yet responded to
Christ. But a dynamically equivalent church will
employ culturally appropriate forms in meeting
these needs--familiar, meaningful forms that it will
possess, adapt, and fill with Christian meanings
(1979:321).

One of the goals of a dynamic-equivalence church would be
to meet the felt needs of that society and stimulate within
it an impact for Christ similar to that which the first century church produced in its day. It would function using
cultural forms which are as indigenous as possible. Kraft
shares an example of dynamic-equivalence from the Nigerian
setting:

In attempting to discover a dynamically equivalent form of preaching I once asked a group of Nigerian church leaders what would be the appropriate way to present a message such as the Christian one to the village council. They replied:

'We would choose the oldest, most respected man in the group and ask him a question. He would discourse, perhaps at length, on the topic and then become silent, whereupon we would ask another question. As the old man talked, other old men would comment as well. But eventually he and the others would do less and less of the talking and the leader would do more and more. In this way we would develop our message and it would become the topic for discussion of the whole village.'

I asked them why they didn't employ this approach in church. 'Why, we've been taught that monologue is the Christian way,' they replied. 'Can this be why no old men come to church?' I asked. 'Of course!' they said. 'We have alienated them all by not showing them due respect in public meetings.' Thus it is that a preaching form that may be appropriate enough in that culture to New Testament models—loses its equivalence when exported to another culture. It becomes counter-productive (1979:322).

Aspects of the dynamic-equivalence model should be applied to all aspects of the church—worship patterns, architecture, organization, leadership, and so forth. The more truly indigenous the church is in its own cultural context the more effective it will be as a dynamic organism for Christ. In this way a bicultural perspective is utilized in the establishment of local churches. Such churches will be solidly rooted in the national culture, and its forms and meanings will reflect a true indigeneity. The potential for growth in dynamic-equivalence churches is great. The Holy Spirit has free course to accomplish His gracious work unhindered by foreign structures imported from outside. The message of the Word of God will be firmly planted within the national framework and expressed in cultural ways which are clearly understood by the people. The same Holy Spirit who functions in our cultures will function in their cultures. The resulting churches will be genuine Christian churches.

Understanding the
Biblical/Theological Dimensions

Some readers have likely been wondering, "What about the Biblical and Theological dimensions in the preparation of missionaries?" Good question. This dimension must not be overlooked. It is indeed foundational and vital in the preparation of cross-cultural workers.

The whole process of how God directs His children into missionary service is a fascinating one to consider. An extended treatment of this subject is beyond the purvey of this manual; however, it may be helpful to recognize that not all prospective missionaries have the same educational background. Many come from evangelical churches where a Bible-based ministry coupled with keen missionary concerns have been emphasized. A large number of these missionaries have continued their education at Bible institutes or Bible colleges. If this has been true, they have been exposed to the Biblical and theological backgrounds for missions.

Other missionaries have experienced limited Bible and missionary exposure in their churches, and later continued their education at Christian liberal arts colleges or at secular colleges and universities. Unless such candidates for missionary service have continued their preparation at evangelical graduate schools or seminaries, their Biblical and theological framework will likely be extremely limited.

Since the clear Biblical basis for missions is an essential for a well trained missionary, it is very important and necessary to include a chapter here regarding these vital

considerations. Most evangelical mission agencies prefer that
their missionaries have at least thirty semester hours of
Bible and theology before proceeding to the field. Sad to
say, some get out to the field without this bare minimum of
Biblical and theological preparation. In order to help fulfill this need in the training of cross-cultural workers this
chapter will attempt to portray a brief Biblical theology of
missions. For an extended treatment of these areas allow me
to refer the reader to two excellent books by J. Herbert Kane:
Christian Missions in Biblical Perspective (Baker, 1976) and
The Christian World Mission: Today and Tomorrow (Baker, 1981).
Also, another recent book with very helpful material is *Per-
spectives On the World Christian Movement: A Reader* edited by
Ralph Winter and Steven Hawthorne and published by William
Carey Library (1981).

Since the whole idea of missions is a Biblical concept
rooted in the heart of a sovereign God, we must consider the
Old Testament and New Testament writings. Our foundations
for ministry in cross-cultural evangelism would be incomplete
without this Biblical background.

THE OLD TESTAMENT AND MISSIONS

Many Christians assume that the missionary enterprise had
its beginnings with our Lord Jesus Christ and His Great Commission. This is incorrect. Such a view completely omits
Jehovah God of the Old Testament. The scarlet thread of God's
wondrous plan for world redemption needs to be seen from the
Old Testament perspective.

A recent writer, Francis M. DuBose, draws attention to
God's gracious activity as "mission means sending." He refers to God as the one who sends and Jesus Christ as the One
who was sent.

> One legitimate and significant approach is
> to begin with a rather universal consensus: mission
> means sending. This is one point on which most
> everyone seems to agree. What better beginning
> point could we have than this kind of consensus?
> And since references to the world mission are
> negligible in our English Bible and since there is
> a rich language of the sending in the Scripture, it
> would appear to be a high agenda item to look care-
> fully at what language conveys in the way of theo-
> logical content. An immediate survey of the term
> sending in its various forms in Scripture suggests

that it is more than a simple descriptive word.
It seems both appropriate and safe, therefore, at
least to begin with the hypothesis that in the sense
of "the sending', there is a biblical idea of mission (DuBose 1983:24).

Yes, this concept helps us to realize the origins of the mis-
sionary enterprise are attributed to God Himself. The Old
Testament reveals the Creator God and His redemptive purpose
for mankind. J. Herbert Kane states it clearly when he writes:
"Jehovah is a missionary God and the Bible is a missionary
Book" (Kane 1981:8).

It may be helpful to see two distinct patterns of missionary activity in the Old Testament. Genesis chapters one and
two reveal Jehovah God as Creator of the universe. In addition, Kane sees "God as the Governor and Judge of the moral
universe, He is the King and Ruler of the Genile nations, and
He is the Father and Redeemer of Israel" (Kane 1976:18-26).

Prior to the Captivity Israel's missionary role may be
seen as "centripetal" -- attraction to a center. Other nations came to Israel but she did not go to them. The nation
Israel, as God's people, attracted other nations to Jehovah
as to a bright light. Isaiah the prophet wrote that Israel
was to be a "light to the nations" (Isaiah 42:6), and he spoke
of God's ultimate purpose which was this: that His salvation
"may reach to the ends of the earth" (Isaiah 9:6). (Kane
1981:26)

After the Captivity and during the period of the Exile,
the missionary role changed. The action became centrifugal
in that Israel went out to other nations. It was like a spin-
off action. A witness was borne and there were attempts at
proselytism of the Gentile nations. The Jewish nation was
dispersed or scattered throughout the Mediterranean world.
They were called the "Diaspora" from the Greek *sperein*, "to
sow," and *dia*, "through or throughout." Hence, their influence and witness were used by God in a missionary sense. God
used Jewish life during the period of the Diaspora as a positive witness to the Gentile nations. J. Herbert Kane summarizes six characteristics of this missionary activity:

1. The institution of the synagogue.
2. The observance of the Sabbath.
3. The translation of the Scriptures from Hebrew into
   Greek which is called the Septuagint.
4. The concept of monotheism.

5. The practice of morality.
6. The promise of a coming Savior: the Messiah!
(Kane 1976:30-33)

As we study the Old Testament it becomes clear that God utilized His people Israel in both centripetal and centrifugal action. God was concerned for both Jew and Gentile. Isaiah records God's direct appeal to the nations: "Turn to me and be saved all the ends of the earth" (Isaiah 45:22). It is obvious that the missionary message is clearly set forth in the Old Testament.

Long ago in Genesis chapter 12 God made a covenant with Abraham. This promise had wide implications and relates to God's purpose in world redemption:

Now the Lord said to Abram, 'Go forth from
your country, and from your relatives and from
your father's house, to the land which I will
show you; and I will make you a great nation, and
I will bless you, and make your name great; and so
you shall be a blessing; and I will bless those
who bless you, and the one who curses you I will
curse. And in you all the families of the earth
shall be blessed' (Genesis 12:1-3, NASB).

We should note in this Abrahamic covenant the last phrase, "And in you all the families of the earth shall be blessed" (Gen. 12:3). How could God bless all the families of the earth through Abraham? It was only possible through Abraham's seed, Jesus Christ. A Redeemer-Savior was promised, and this was not fulfilled until the coming of Jesus Christ. It was through HIM that great blessing would come! It is noteworthy that both Mary in her "magnificat" (Luke 1:46-55) and Zacharias, the father of John the Baptist, refer to God's promise to Abraham (Like 2:67-79, esp. v. 72). The birth of our Lord Jesus Christ was clearly a fulfillment of God's promise to Abraham hundreds of years before. These considerations now lead us to the New Testament. Here the clearest theology of missions emerges.

THE NEW TESTAMENT AND MISSIONS

While it is true that the seeds of the missionary movement are found in the Old Testament, the full blossom may be seen in the New Testament. The concept of a promised deliverer-- the Messiah--originates in the Old Testament, but the fulfillment of that promise is found in the New Testament.

Matthew, Mark, Luke and John all bear witness to that fulfillment. The life, teachings, death, and resurrection of
Jesus Christ are all central to the missionary message.
Sometimes it is helpful to use a simple diagram to illustrate the basic theology of missions as depicted in the New
Testament. Through the experience of many years I have
often shared the diagram below with my students.

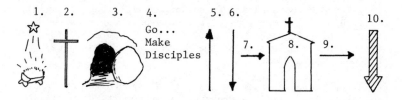

Each part of the diagram is an integral part of the unfolding
of God's redemptive plan for the ages. An understanding of
these events will underline the necessity of the missionary
enterprise. Let's look at the diagram in greater detail.

1. *The Incarnation.* The first simple diagram represents the
manger scene where Jesus Christ was born in Bethlehem of
Judea. The star shining above is the visible sign which the
Magi from the East followed as they journeyed to the place
where the Christ was born (Matt. 2:1-11). The Old Testament
prophets had foretold His birth. Micah had written: "But as
for you, Bethlehem Ephrathah, too little to be among the
clans of Judea, from you One will go forth for Me to be ruler
in Israel. His goings forth are from long ago, from the days
of eternity" (Micah 5:2, NASB).

His virgin birth had been heralded by Isaiah seven hundred years before that great event occurred: "Therefore the
Lord Himself will give you a sign: Behold, a virgin will be
with child and bear a son, and she will call His name Imman-
uel" (Isaiah 7:14, NASB). Concerning His greatness the angel
Gabriel appeared to the virgin Mary and declared:

> . . . 'Hail, favored one! The Lord is with
> you'. . . . 'Do not be afraid, Mary; for you have
> found favor with God. And behold, you will con-
> ceive in your womb, and bear a son, and you shall
> name Him Jesus. He will be great, and will be
> called the Son of the Most High; and the Lord God
> will give Him the throne of His father David; and
> He will reign over the house of Jacob for ever; and
> His Kingdom will have no end' (Luke 1:28-33, NASB).

The purpose of His coming was revealed and His Person was clearly identified when the angel appeared to the shepherds: "And the angel said to them, 'Do not be afraid; for behold I bring you good news of a great joy which shall be for all the people; for today in the city of David there has been born for you a Savior, who is Christ the Lord'" (Luke 2:10-11, NASB). God's promise of a Redeemer-Savior was realized in the birth of His Son, Jesus Christ. The word incarnation means that God became flesh and lived among men. In John's Gospel we read, "And the Word became flesh, and dwelt among us, and we beheld His glory, glory as of the only begotten from the Father, full of grace and truth" (John 1"14, NASB). Yes, His purpose in coming was to be the Savior, and He was none other than God's beloved Son.

A few years later in the historical record the Apostle Paul testified: "It is a trustworthy statement, deserving full acceptance, that Christ Jesus came into the world to save sinners, among whom I am foremost of all" (I Timothy 1:15 NASB). The Son of God who came to be the Savior of the world was born that first Christmas morning. The implications of that miraculous birth are significant in the development of a theology of missions. Normally babies are born to live, but here was a Son who was born to die.

2. *The Crucifixion.* The central theme of the Christian message focuses upon the significance of the cross. During His earthly life and ministry Jesus taught His disciples concerning His impending death. Matthew gives an example of this. Following the feeding of the 4,000 (Matt. 15) and the asking of that fateful question of Peter, "But who do you say that I am?" (Matt. 16:15), Matthew records: "From that time Jesus Christ began to show His disciples that He must go to Jerusalem, and suffer many things from the elders and chief priests and scribes, and be killed, and be raised up on the third day" (Matt. 16:21, NASB).

This was shocking news to impetuous Peter who objected strongly to Jesus' revelation. Nevertheless, Jesus reminded Peter of God's purposes for Himself and fixed His eyes toward the cross. John's Gospel presents the great purpose and love of God in sending His Son to earth. "For God so loved the world, that He gave His only begotten Son, that whoever believes in Him should not perish, but have eternal life" (John 3:16, NASB).

When Paul wrote to the church at Rome he emphasized the significance of Christ's death. "But God demonstrates His own love toward us, in that while we were yet sinners, Christ died for us" (Rom. 5:8, NASB). The death of Christ upon the cross meant that forgiveness of sins could be granted because of the atoning work of the Savior. Jesus Himself declared "that repentance for forgiveness of sins should be proclaimed in His name to all the nations, beginning from Jerusalem" (Luke 24:47 NASB). This knowledge of forgiveness of sins was to be shared with all nations. This fact alone should motivate us to proclaim the Good News to the ends of the earth!

In our complacent, self-sufficient age, it is so easy to relax and think the benefits of the Gospel are just for us here in North America. No, this is false! The benefits of the sacrifice of Christ are for the whole world--for all peoples! John reminds us of this implication: ". . . and He Himself is the propitiation for our sins; and not for ours only, but also for those of the whole world" (I John 2:2, NASB). Yes, the cross and all that it means is integral to our theology of missions. Without it there would be no Good News to proclaim!

3. *The Resurrection of Christ.* Our Lord Jesus Christ did not remain upon the cross. He was buried in a borrowed tomb, but on the third day He arose from the dead! The third diagram attempts to portray the stone rolled away from the tomb. Matthew records the event of the women coming to the tomb on that first Easter morning:

> And the angel answered and said to the women, 'Do not be afraid; for I know that you are looking for Jesus who has been crucified. He is not here, for He has risen, just as He said; come, see the place where He was lying. And go quickly and tell His disciples that He has risen from the dead; and behold, He is going before you into Galilee; there you will see Him; behold, I have told you' (Matt. 28:5-7, NASB).

Peter and John witnessed the empty tomb (John 20). Jesus appeared to Mary (Jn. 20:14-17) and also to the disciples (Jn. 20:19-21). Later He appeared to more than five hundred others (I Cor. 15:6).

The significance of the resurrection of Jesus Christ is unique in annals of religious writings. No other founder of a religion has ever claimed to rise again from the dead. This fact alone sets Jesus Christ apart from all other religious leaders. Without the resurrection of our Lord Jesus

Christ the Christian message would lack an authoritative message to proclaim. The Apostle Paul staked his entire ministry on the veracity of Christ's resurrection:

> . . . and if Christ has not been raised, then our preaching is vain, and your faith also is vain. Moreover we are even found to be false witnesses of God, because we witness against God that He raised Christ, whom He did not raise, if in fact the dead are not raised. For if the dead are not raised, not even Christ has been raised; and if Christ has not been raised, your faith is worthless; you are still in your sins (I Cor. 15:14-17, NASB).

Our Christian faith rests upon the veracity of the Gospel accounts concerning the resurrection. Paul affirms that the cross and the resurrection of Christ are essential doctrines of our theology of missions. "He was delivered over to death for our sins and was raised to life for our justification" (Rom. 4:25, NIV). Praise God!

4. *The Great Commission*. The next major event in our theology of missions is the ascension of our Lord, but something happened just prior to His return to the father. Jesus shared a very important message with His disciples before He ascended to glory. This message is called "the Great Commission," and it has been a significant command in the history of the Christian movement. All four Gospel writers draw attention to these challenging words of our Lord, and the book of Acts contains a fifth reiteration. The accounts in the Gospels of Mark and John are very brief while Matthew and Luke include more information. Our Lord declared:

> . . . 'All authority has been given to Me in heaven and on earth. God therefore and make disciples of all nations, baptizing them in the name of the Father and the Son and the Holy Spirit, teaching them to observe all that I commanded you; and lo, I am with you always, even to the end of the age' (Matt. 28:18-20, NASB).

> And He said to them, 'God into all the world and preach the Gospel to all creation' (Mark 16:15).

> . . . 'Thus it is written, that the Christ should suffer and rise again from the dead the third day; and that repentance for forgiveness

of sins should be proclaimed in His name to all
the nations, beginning from Jerusalem. You are
witnesses of these things' (Luke 24:46-48, NASB).

Jesus therefore said to them again, 'Peace
be with you; as the Father has sent Me, I also
send you' *John 20:21, NASB).

But you shall receive power when the Holy
Spirit has come upon you; and you shall be My
witnesses both in Jerusalem, and in all Judea
and Samaria, and even to the remotest part of
the earth (Acts 1:8, NASB).

It would appear that the Holy Spirit had inspired the
Gospel writers to repeat the Great Commission five times for
our learning! There have been times in the history of the
church when the Great Commission of our Lord was interpreted
by some (1500 - 1800 A.D.) to refer to the first century disciples alone; hence, the momentum of missions was temporarily
stifled. Following the time of William Carey in England--
after 1972--a renewed emphasis upon the applicability of
our Lord's Great Commission for all generations was established. Giant missionary strides were taken in the nineteenth century. A careful reading of church history since
1792 will reveal that where obedience to the Great Commission
has been exercised the church has grown and expanded on all
continents.

In fact, the major part of the New Testament writings is
attributable to a fulfillment of the Great Commission. The
Pauline Epistles were written to mission churches. Robert
Hall Glover drew attention to this when he wrote:

To use the words of Professor W. O. Carver:
'If there had been no Commission, or no obedience
to its spirit, there would have been no need for
the New Testament writings and no occasion for
their production. A product of missions, the New
Testament can be truly interpreted only in the
light of the missionary idea' (Glover 1946:22).

These weighty words of commission from the lips of our Lord
just prior to His ascension have always been a challenge to
the church in every age. They continue to speak to us today.
The contemporary church must be involved in "making disciples
of all nations" (Matt. 28:19). This task will involve us in
cross-cultural ministry as we obey our Lord and Master by

taking the Gospel to the ends of the earth.

5. *The Ascension.* The words of the Great Commission were no sooner out of the lips of Christ when He suddenly ascended to the Father. Luke records the event in Acts 1:9: "And after He had said these things, He was lifted up while they were looking on, and a cloud received Him out of their sight" (NASB). It is easy to omit the ascension of Christ in considering a theology of missions. Quite often it is dismissed in a sentence or two. It is very instructive to note the missionary implications of our Lord's ascension.

First, it clearly confirmed the fact of the ascension. The earthly sojourn of our Lord was temporary. By His own admission He came "to seek and to save that which was lost" (Luke 19:10, NASB). Jesus Himself summarized His mission when He said: "I came forth from the Father, and have come into the world; I am leaving the world again, and going to the Father" (John 16:28, NASB). It is clear He anticipated His return to heaven. When the event occurred, it marked the close of His earthly ministry.

Secondly, the angels who spoke at the ascension foretold His second coming. Luke records their message:

> And as they were gazing intently into the sky while He was departing, behold, two men in white clothing stood beside them; and they also said, 'Men of Galilee, why do you stand looking into the sky? This Jesus, who has been taken from you into heaven, will come in just the same way as you have watched Him go into heaven' (Acts 1:10-11, NASB).

Here is a promise that this same Jesus will return to earth. In the meantime He has given His church a task worldwide. There is more to be said regarding our Lord's return as it too is an integral part of our theology of missions.

A third missionary implication relates to the timing of the coming of the Holy Spirit. The Holy Spirit could not come until our Lord had ascended to the Father. Jesus had instructed His disciples about this fact, although at the time they likely understood little about what He said. John has preserved our Lord's words as He tried to prepare His disciples for that which was coming later: "But I tell you the truth, it is to your advantage that I go away; for if I do not go away, the Helper shall not come to you; but if I go,

I will send Him to you" (John 16:7, NASB).

Yes, our Lord's ascent to the Father paved the way for the coming of the Holy Spirit. 'At the ascension the curtain dropped on His earthly life; after that His followers were called on to live by faith, not by sight' (Kane 1976:219).

6. *Pentecost: the Descent of the Holy Spirit.* The sixth aspect in our pictorial summary of a theology of missions is an arrow pointing downward. This signifies the coming of the Holy Spirit at Pentecost. It is one of the great and outstanding events in the New Testament. Concerning this occurrence Kane states:

> The most important event recorded in the Acts of the Apostles is the coming of the Holy Spirit at Pentecost. That event overshadows all others. Without it all the other wonderful happenings would be without adequate explanation. Indeed, without Pentecost the other events would never have taken place (Kane 1976:227).

Our Lord had promised that the Holy Spirit would come following His crucifixion and resurrection (John 16:7). He said the Holy Spirit would be sent by the Father in His name (John 14:26), but later He spoke of the Holy Spirit "whom I will send to you from the Father, that is the Spirit of truth. . ." (John 15:26). It seems clear that both the Father and the Son were involved in the sending of the third person of the trinity. Furthermore, Jesus defined the role of the Holy Spirit in ministry:

> And He, when He comes, will convict the world concerning sin, and righteousness, and judgment; concerning sin, because they do not believe in Me; and concerning righteousness, because I go to the Father, and you no longer behold Me; and concerning judgment, because the ruler of this world has been judged (John 16:8-11, NASB).

These are weighty words and they relate to a theology of missions directly. The convicting and converting work of God in human lives is performed by the Holy Spirit. Jesus taught that the Holy Spirit "will teach you all things. . ." (John 14:26), "He will bear witness of Me. . ." (John 15:26), "He will guide you into all the truth. . ." (John 16:13), and "He shall glorify Me. . ." (John 16:14).

Kane draws attention to three new things that were instituted at Pentecost: the inauguration of a new age -- the
age of the Holy Spirit; the formation of a new organism: the
Christian church; and the beginning of a new movement: the
worldwide missionary movement (Kane, 1976:242). Each of these
new realities is an exciting development.

The coming of the Holy Spirit at Pentecost was directly
concerned with stimulating this new missionary movement.
Acts chapter two records the account. There were unusual manifestations that day. Things like "a rushing wind," "tongues
of fire," and "they were all filled with the Holy Spirit and
began to speak with other tongues, as the Spirit gave them
utterance" (Acts 2:2-4). What was the reason for this
startling event? The multitude which had gathered were
amazed, "because they were each one hearing them speak in
his own language" (Acts 2:6).

They were amazed because they knew the disciples present
were Galileans, and yet they recognized languages spoken all
around the Mediterreanean world (see Acts 2:8-11). The key
to understanding the significance of this event is found in
Acts 2:11: "we hear them in our own tongues speaking of the
mighty deeds of God." What were these mighty deeds?

If we just think back a few weeks prior to Pentecost, it
is not too difficult to recall that the two "mighty deeds"
which had just occurred were the crucifixion of our Lord and
His glorious resurrection! These were the "mighty deeds of
God" which, in His sovereign purpose, He desired to make
known to these representatives from all over the then known
world.

They were without T.V., radio, telephones, and the
printing press which we take so much for granted in our
present age. God performed a mighty miracle in sending His
Holy Spirit to enable the disciples to bear witness to His
beloved Son. God was laying the groundwork for the great
missionary movement to follow. Thus, we see the dynamic
significance of the coming of the Holy Spirit in a Biblical
theology of missions.

7. *The arrow pointing outward: witness*! The Pentecost event
provided the power needed for witness; hence, the book of
Acts illustrates for us how the missionary movement gained
momentum. There is a sense in which Acts 1:8 provides an
excellent table of contents for what happened in the book of
Acts. These were the words of Jesus just before His ascension

to the Father, and they represent the fifth recounting of the
Great Commission in the New Testament:

> But you shall receive power when the Holy
> Spirit has come upon you; and you shall be My
> witnesses both in Jerusalem, and in all Judea
> and Samaria, and even to the remotest part of
> the earth (Acts 1:8, NASB).

If we study carefully, we may note that in Acts chapters
one to seven the witness of the disciples to their Lord was
generally in the Jerusalem area. In chapters eight to twelve
the witness and ministry expanded to include Samaria located
to the north from Jerusalem. Then, from Acts thirteen to the
end of the book the witness blossomed throughout Asia Minor
and into southern Europe through the dynamic ministry of the
Apostle Paul. Thus, it may be seen that the challenge our
Lord gave in Acts 1:8 was initially fulfilled in the first
century by the early church. It was their desire to extend
the Gospel to the "ends of the earth." Just so, in our age
we should be doing the same.

The witness was presented to both Jew and Gentile, and
at times prejudicial feelings between these two cultural
groups had to be overcome. It is exciting to realize that
the early disciples were obedient to their Lord. Peter min-
istered to Jews, and Philip shared with Samaritans. Paul and
Barnabas with Silas, Timothy and Luke had the job of extend-
ing the Good News "to the remotest part of the earth." Recognizing these early beginnings of this missionary obedience is
essential in our understanding of a Biblical theology of missions. Our next concern will be to consider the results of
that dynamic witness of the first century disciples.

8. *"I will build my church."* When our Lord gave His Great
Commission challenging His disciples "to make disciples of
all nations" (Mt. 28:19), He told them: "you shall be My
witnesses. . ." (Acts 1:8). For what purpose was this witness to be performed? During His earthly ministry Jesus
had made known four startling predictions. Concerning
these Kane comments:

> Jesus made four great declarations: I will
> rise again; I will send My Spirit; I will build
> My church; I will come again. The first two are
> already accomplished facts. The third is now
> going on. And the fourth is yet to come (Kane
> 1976:226).

Yes, our Lord made the bold assertion: ". . . I will build my church; and the gates of Hades shall not overpower it" (Matt. 16:18). After the Holy Spirit's descent at Pentecost, this work of building His church commenced in earnest.

Through the witness of the disciples in Jerusalem numbers of local assemblies of believers came into being. A strong church emerged at Antioch in the north, and this became a strong missionary church. Its most notable missionary pioneer was Saul who later became the fearless Paul, the Apostle. That Paul took the task of church planting seriously is quite obvious from the reading of Acts chapter thirteen onwards. Wherever Paul preached--whether in Ephesus, Colosse, Philippi,ι, Thessalonica, or Corinth--there were those who believed and turned in faith to Jesus Christ.

These churches were composed of groups of believers in the Lord Jesus Christ. The word we translate "church" is loaded with meaning. Let's not confues it with mere buildings! It is composed of two Greek words, *"ekklesia"--ek* means "out of" and *kaleo* means "to call." Hence, the "church" in ef-effect is really groups of "called out ones." They have been called out of the world and its sinful ways to become a part of that "new organism"--the CHURCH! Here believers would learn to worship, hear and teach the Scriptures, and learn to witness and serve our Lord Jesus Christ. A Biblical theology of missions must include "ecclesiology"--the doctrine of the church. We come to step nine in the diagram we've been considering.

9. *The Church Age.* The church had its roots and beginnings in the book of Acts. Early Christians carried the Gospel message far and near, and often there was severe persecution and suffering for the cause of Christ. The arrow (in Figure 6) continues pointing outward. This represents the on-going task of missions and church planting.

It would be beyond the purvey of this brief summary of a theology of missions to attempt to capsulize the history of the Christian movement down through the ages. Others have done this and the books are available for our learning.

The work of the church and missions has always been opposed. Satan delights to hinder and destroy the work of God wherever it may be found. The rise of Islam in the seventh century A.D. dealt a severe blow to the North African church and to the entire Middle Eastern area. Likewise Communism is a contemporary foe.

There were dark days when the Gospel light grew dim. Sin and corruption affected the church as did cultural, theological, and geographical divisions. The coming of the Reformation under Martin Luther re-ignited a spark which is continuing today under the banner of Protestant missions. The introduction of sin, selfishness, and pride have often attacked the church. Theological liberalism has eroded the firm Biblical basis of missions. Yet God has graciously sent revival and renewal upon His church periodically in order to cleanse and revitalize it. For this gracious work we should be profoundly thankful!

One of the exciting dimensions in missions today is the rise of the Third World Church. God is raising up Third World missionaries in the developing nations, and He is helping them to form new mission agencies to send these missionaries out. Recent research by Lawrence E. Keyes, now president of Overseas Crusades, was cited by C. Peter Wagner in *On the Crest Of the Wave:*

> The international survey done by Wong, Pentecost, and Larson in 1972 identified 3,404 workers serving under 203 third-world sending agencies. Larry Keyes's 1980 update listed 368 agencies sending over 13,000 missionaries in 1980, conservatively projected to over 15,000 by the end of 1981. If that rate of increase continues, the third-world Protestant missionary force may · project to over 50,000 by the end of the century (Wagner 1983:171).

Third World Christians are accepting missionary responsibilities seriously. It is exciting to see their obedience to the Great Commission. The Church Age would be incomplete without their sacrificial participation. We in the West must link arms with them by prayer, financial assistance, and whole-hearted encouragement. The close of this age of grace may be fast approaching!

10. *The Return of Christ.* The large arrow pointing downwards represents the second coming of Christ. A Biblical theology of missions would not be complete without the promised return of our Lord. There is an eschatological dimension to the missionary enterprise. What God has commenced He is able to bring to a logical consummation.

Jesus Himself predicted His return to earth. In John's Gospel we read:

> Let not your heart be troubled; believe in
> God, believe also in Me. In My Father's house
> are many dwelling places; if it were not so, I
> would have told you; for I go to prepare a place
> for you. And if I go and prepare a place for you,
> I will come again, and receive you to Myself;
> that where I am, there you may be also (John
> 14:1-3, NASB).

At the time of His ascension the two angels also spoke of
His return: "Men of Galilee, who do you stand looking into
the sky? This Jesus, who has been taken up from you into
heaven, will come in just the same way as you have watched
Him go into heaven" (Acts 1:11 NASB). In the meantime we
live in the church age--an age of grace. Kane reminds us
of the church's chief responsibility:

> The church which He founded is a historical
> institution. It had its beginning at Pentecost
> and will run its course until the Second Advent.
> Between these two points the chief task of the
> church is to proclaim the universal lordship of
> Jesus Christ, helping in this way to prepare
> for His return. This task was given to the church
> by her Lord. The mandate is clear: Preach the
> gospel to every creature; make disciples of all
> nations; occupy till I come (Kane 1976:251).

The New Testament speaks to us about terminal goals for
the church and the missionary movement. One refers to the
end of the age. Jesus referred to it in Matthew 28:20,
". . . lo, I am with you always, even to the end of the age."
Here our Lord promised His presence with His servants until
the end of this age.

The other goal relates to geography. In the Acts 1:8
account of the Great Commission after Jesus had mentioned
being His witnesses in Jerusalem, Judea, and Samaria, He
added, "and unto the uttermost parts of the earth." How can
we relate these two terminal goals: the end of the age and
the uttermost parts of the earth?

Our Lord's words in Matthew chapter 24 will help us to
understand the relationship of these goals. In the earlier
part of the chapter (Matt. 24:3) the disciples approached
Jesus and asked, "Tell us, when will these things be, and
what will be the sign of your coming and of the end of the
age?" They were concerned about eschatology as many

Christians are today. Part of Jesus's answer included the proclamation of the Gospel worldwide. He replied: "And this gospel of the kingdom shall be preached in the whole world for a witness to all the nations, and then the end shall come" (Matthew 24:14 NASB). Here is a very clear passage of Scripture in the very words of our Lord which directly relates Christ's second coming with the on-going missionary movement.

Matthew 24:14 speaks to us about a message, a mission, and a motive. The message is the "gospel of the kingdom"—Good News about the King, Jesus Christ. The Incarnation, the Crucifixion, and the Resurrection, as well as the Great Commission are all a part of the Good News.

The mission, Jesus said, was that this gospel of the kingdom "shall be preached in the whole world for a witness. . ." This has always been the mission and the marching orders for the church. The motive is that reminder by our Lord Himself that after the gospel of the kingdom has been preached in the whole world for a witness to all the nations, "and then the end shall come." Here is a clear motivation from our Lord Himself to continue with the great task of world evangelization, for only when that task is complete will our Lord return. George Eldon Ladd in his helpful book, *The Blessed Hope*, affirms that "Christ is tarrying until the church has completed its task. When Matthew 24:14 has been fulfilled, then Christ will come" (Ladd 1956:148).

There are some who hold to a view of eschatology which teaches that Christ may come at any moment—even today. On the basis of Matthew 24:14 we must conclude that if our Lord returns today, tomorrow, or next week, the gospel of the kingdom will have been preached in the whole world for a witness to all the nations. However, if He does not return today, tomorrow, next week, or next year, the church of Jesus Christ has an unfinished task to be accomplished until that great day comes.

God, the Father, alone knows that day. Meanwhile let us be faithful to our Lord as we understand a Biblical theology of missions. Let's accept our Lord's challenge: "Therefore beseech the Lord of the harvest to send out workers into His harvest" (Matthew 9:38, NASB).

Conclusions

Preparing missionaries for the complex task of intercultural communication is not a simple matter. The missionary enterprise spans the entire world and involves relationships with approximately four and one-half billion people.
These billions of people are comprised of a great diversity
of nationalities and groups. The ethnic diversity is extremely complex. The magnitude of the task is staggering.
Yet, we are challenged by the declaration of the Lord of the
harvest: "I will build my church, and the gates of Hades
will not overcome it" (Matthew 16:18 NIV). This enormous
endeavor has been committed by our Lord to His church--the
people of God--all over the world.

The weighty demands of the missionary task challenge us
to prepare and train the best missionaries possible to engage
in world evangelization. Missionaries do not just appear
automatically. They must be carefully prepared and trained
for their task. As a result of training better prepared missionaries, I would like to suggest that we should expect the
following benefits in completing the task of world evangelization:

1. Missionaries will be in a better position to understand the peoples to whom they go with the Good News. Missionaries who are trained from a bicultural perspective will
be more sensitive to the needs of others in a cross-cultural
context. They will not simply assume that the nationals of
the host country are the same or similar to themselves. They
will be aware of cultural difference. The missionary will

see the nationals of whatever country as valid persons within
their own cultural setting. The importance of their social
structure will be recognized, and the missionary will seek to
work within that structure.

In seeking to accept the nationals as they are and attempting to understand them more completely, the missionary
will be building bridges of mutual respect. When good rapport
with people is established, then trust relationships may be
built. Such an understanding of people will pave the way for
the ministries of proclamation and conversion.

2. Missionaries will be better communicators of the Gospel in cross-cultural contexts. It is common for young, inexperienced missionaries to wonder if they will ever be able
to communicate in the new language. At times there may come
a lack of inner peace and satisfaction regarding their missionary endeavor. The missionary who has been trained to
think and act biculturally will be in a better position to
communicate the Good News.

Recognizing the need for adequate language learning, the
new missionary should approach language learning positively
with a desire to learn the language from native speakers and
to learn it well. This is demanding and time consuming;
nevertheless, good language facility is foundational for all
that follows. Without it there is no effective communication.

Closely aligned with language learning is the desire for
culture learning. Having been prepared for culture shock,
the new missionary is in a better position to minimize it.
Its manifestations will be recognized and steps toward overcoming it can be taken.

The importance of worldview will be recognized. As the
missionary attempts to introduce the Gospel message, he/she
should be aware of the prevailing worldview of the people.
This awareness alone will help to avoid distortions and misunderstandings among the people as they seek to understand
and apply the Christian message. It may be necessary to alter
or adjust evangelistic approaches so that they are more compatible with the worldview of the receptor people. In this
way the best interests of good communication will be served,
and the result will be improved understanding of the rele-
vancy of the message.

The bicultural missionary will recognize the importance
of understanding the dynamics of culture change. The

missionary's role as an agent of change--both religious and
otherwise--should be recognized. Thus, in the communication
of the Christian message the missionary will be alert to the
dynamics which are operating within the cultural system. The
Holy Spirit guides and enables missionaries to work within
the parameters of the existing system. Change will be in-
evitable wherever the Gospel is introduced; however, the way
in which change is effected may determine the success or
failure of God's work.

At times there may be aspects of the nationals' worldview
which are opposed to biblical revelation. Working with national believers and depending upon the Holy Spirit and the
Word of God, the missionary should seek to introduce the
necessary changes. It is far better when respected leaders
of the people become the innovators for change; nevertheless,
the missionary may be the catalyst in that process. Usually
this process will be accomplished quietly, without fanfare,
and in cooperation with the natural leaders.

3. Missionaries will be less ethnocentric and more appre-
ciative of national believers and their culture. Just being
aware of ethnocentrism and its dangers is a significant aid
for the missionary. If the missionary insists on doing everything the same way it is done in his homeland, then barriers
may be erected that will hinder the progress of evangelization. However, when the missionary recognizes that there are
other ways of doing things and does not impose his ethnocentric ways, the Holy Spirit is free to accomplish the work of
conviction and conversion. Missionaries, if they are adequately trained for cross-cultural ministry, will seek to
facilitate rather than hinder the Holy Spirit's work. Sad
to say, some missionaries never come to the place where they
recognize their ethnocentric tendencies. Biculturally
trained missionaries are in a much better position to avoid
ethnocentrism and the cultural imperialism that may easily
follow.

The contemporary phenomena of Third World missions is a
refreshing trend. It has come like a breath of fresh air.
National churches that were formerly recipients of the Gospel
are now sending out missionaries to other nations. In 1973
it was estimated that there were about 3,000 Third World
missionaries throughout the world. Research in 1980 indicates that there are at least 8,315 (and likely many more!)
Third World missionaries being sent out by 430 missionary
societies (*Church Growth Bulletin*, Sept./Oct. 1980:55).

The role of the missionary has changed in many of these lands. No longer is the Western missionary the "great white father" who runs the whole show. Today missionaries are received as co-laborers with national brethren, and often under the direction and authority of the national church. Ethnocentric attitudes have no place in this new arrangement. Missionaries who can appreciate and strengthen their national brethren and build bridges of mutual respect will be in demand in the years ahead. Missionaries from all nations are partners in obedience to fulfill the Great Commission.

4. Better preparation of missionaries will reduce potential "dropouts." Many mission leaders are concerned about missionary dropouts. There are many variables that cause such attrition. One of the important keys, often overlooked, is inadequate preparation for the missionary task. A missionary who has not been adequately prepared cannot be expected to become a successful missionary in a cross-cultural context. Missionaries with only minimal cross-cultural preparation, or none at all, easily become discouraged and defeated; hence, they withdraw from the field and return home. They are often dubbed "dropouts" and learn to live with this stigma. Some find it difficult to face confrontation with home churches and Christian friends; so, they move to a new area and attempt to make a fresh start in life. This pattern has been repeated again and again. Would better missionary preparation be a help?

Missionaries who are trained both spiritually and biculturally are in a stronger position to function as effective missionaries wherever the Lord may lead them. It is my firm conviction that the dropout rate can be reduced considerably by adequately preparing missionaries for cross-cultural communication. Missionary service is a demanding vocation; hence, God's servants deserve the finest preparation available--both spiritually and cross-culturally--in order that they might succeed in their ministry.

5. Biculturally trained missionaries are better prepared to engage in the planting of dynamic equivalence churches. Church planting and development are key priorities of missionary endeavor. Missionaries who have had the benefit of anthropology training, coupled with principles of cross-cultural communication are more alert to establish churches that make an impact similar to that of churches in the first century. It will not be their desire to plant churches that are copies of the North American variety. Biculturally prepared missionaries will encourage growth and creativity on

the part of nationals to establish truly indigenous churches utilizing national leadership, resources, and ways of doing things.

Church planting and church growth will be chief priorities. Other types of missionary endeavor will be subservient to these primary tasks of Christian mission. This vision is to be passed on to key national believers so that they too become involved in that great task concerning which the Apostle Paul exhorted Timothy: "And the things you have heard me say in the presence of many witnesses entrust to reliable men who will also be qualified to teach others" (II Timothy 2:2 NIV). Strong and vibrant national churches are better able to evangelize their own people, and they will do so as the Holy Spirit motivates them to proclaim the Gospel and to establish churches. Thus missionaries will be freed to assist as catalysts in other needy areas as co-workers together with the national brethren.

6. Better initial preparation of missionaries will pave the way for continuing education in missiological studies. Biculturally trained missionaries function better on the field, and they often have the joy of training others. Generally it is their desire to persevere in the work of God over a period of many years. During their furloughs such missionaries may wish to sharpen their tools and keep abreast of new developments in missionary techniques and methodologies. The field of missions, now called Missiology, is rapidly coming into its own and its insights are helping the missionary task all over the world.

Missionaries who have had a foundation in cross-cultural communication and who have worked abroad for some years may wish to pursue graduate work in missiology. Continuing education can also help them greatly in the development of cross-cultural ministries. A number of schools now offer courses in missiology which lead to the master's and doctoral levels. Among these schools are the School of World Mission at Fuller Theological Seminary (Pasadena, CA), and School of World Mission and Evangelism at Trinity Evangelical Divinity School (Deerfield, IL), both offering doctoral programs in Missiology. Several other schools offering missiology courses at the master's level are Columbia Bible College Graduate School of Bible and Missions (Columbia, SC), Wheaton Graduate School (Wheaton, IL), and Canadian Theological College (Regina, SK Canada). Numerous other graduate schools offer helpful missions courses. Opportunities abound for furloughing missionaries to become better equipped for the task of missions today.

Many mission boards recognize the need for advanced training and encourage their workers to continue their education
in missions. This is a healthy trend and such missions
should be commended. Furloughing missionaries should investigate these opportunities and avail themselves of advanced
missiological education. Cross-cultural ministry demands
the best trained personnel possible for the accomplishment
of the Great Commission. While it is true that great zeal,
dedication, and sacrifice are still needed today, yet adequately prepared missionaries will greatly facilitate the
worldwide advance of the Gospel.

Missionary work requires diligent workers who understand
the world in which they live. The Good News to be proclaimed
must be communicated clearly and carefully in cross-cultural
contexts all over the world. In order to accomplish this
great task bicultural missionaries are a necessity. They
must be trained and prepared well. As they go forth in obedience to Jesus Christ and filled with the Holy Spirit, God
will bless their ministry with the multiplication of national
churches on every continent. May it ever be so to the praise
and honor of His glory!

Bibliography

Alli, Billiamin A.
   1975   "Acculturation in a Post Traditional Society."
            Missiology, Vol. 3, No. 1

Arndt, J. Richard, and Lindquist, Stanley
   1976   "Twenty to Fifty Percent Fail to Make It--Why?"
            Evangelical Missions Quarterly, Vol. 12, No. 3.

Barnett, Homer G.
   1953   *Innovation: The Basis of Cultural Change*, New
            York: McGraw-Hill Book Co.

Barney, G. Linwood, and Larson, Donald N.
   1967   "How We Can Lick the Language Problem." *Evan-
            gelical Missions Quarterly*, Vol. 4, No. 1.

Bates, Gerald E.
   1979   "Whose Problem Is This, Anyhow?" *Evangelical
            Missions Quarterly*, Vol. 15, No. 1.

   1977   "Who Is Qualified to be Called a Missionary?"
            Evangelical Missions Quarterly, Vol. 13, No. 4.

   1980   "Missions and Cross-Cultural Conflict."
            Missiology, Vol. 8, No. 1.

Beaver, R. Pierce
   1973   *The Gospel and Frontier Peoples*, So. Pasadena,
            CA: Wm. Carey Library.

Beals, Alan R.
    1967   *Culture In Process.* New York: Holt, Rinehart
            and Winston.

Bee, Robert L.
    1974   *Patterns and Processes.* New York: The Free Press.

Bialystok, Ellen
    1978   "A Theoretical Model of Second Language Learning."
            Language Learning, Vol. 28, No. 1.

Blanchard, Wendell
    1958   *Thailand: Its People, Its Society, Its Culture.*
            New Haven: Hraf Press.

Bock, Philip K.
    1974   *Modern Cultural Anthropology.* 2nd ed., New York:
            Alfred A. Knopf.

Brewster, E. Thomas and Brewster, Elizabeth S.
    1980   "Bonding and the Missionary Task." Unpublished
            manuscript, School of World Mission, Fuller
            Theological Seminary.

    1980   "Language Learning Midwifery." *Missiology*, Vol.
            8, No. 2.

    1978   "Involvement as a Means of Second Culture Learn-
            ing." *Readings in Missionary Anthropology II.*
            Edited by William A. Smalley, Pasadena, CA: Wm.
            Carey Library.

    1976   *Language Acquisition Made Practical.* Colorado
            Springs, CO: Lingua House.

Brown, Arthur Judson
    1950   *The Foreign Missionary, Today, and Yesterday.*
            New York: Revell.

Bryant, David
    1979   *In the Gap: What It Means To Be a World Chris-
            tian.* Madison, Wisconsin: Inter-Varsity Press.

Buker, Raymond B., Sr.
    1964   "Missionary Encounter With Culture." *Evangel-
            ical Missions Quarterly*, Vol. 1, No. 1

Castillo, Metosalem Q.
    1976   *Missiological Education: A Proposed Curriculum.*
            M.A. Thesis School of World Mission, Fuller
            Theological Seminary.

Chang, Joseph J.
    1976   *An Introduction to Missiology.* Unpublished
            doctoral dissertation, School of World Mission,
            Fuller Theological Seminary.

Coggins, Wade T.
    1966   "Whither the Short-Termer?" *Evangelical Missions
            Quarterly,* Vol. 3, No. 3.

Coots, David L.
    1976   "What To Do About Those New Missionary Frustra-
            tions." *Evangelical Missions Quarterly,* Vol. 12,
            No. 4.

Costas, Orlando E.
    1974   *The Church and Its Mission: A Shattering Cri-
            tique From the Third World.* Wheaton, IL: Tyndale
            House.

    1979   *The Integrity of Mission: The Inner Life and
            Outreach of the Church.* San Francisco: Harper
            & Row.

Dayton, Edward R.
    1980   *That Everyone May Hear,* Monrovia, CA: Missions
            Advanced Research & Communications Center.

Dayton, Edward R., and Fraser, David A.
    1980   *Planning Strategies for World Evangelization.*
            Grand Rapids: Wm. B. Eerdmans Publishing Co.

Deer, Donald S.
    1975   "The Missionary Language-Learning Problem."
            Missiology, Vol. 3, No. 1.

DuBose, Francis M.
    1983   *God Who Sends.* Nashville, Tenn.: Broadman Press.

Dye, T. Wayne
    1974   "Stress Producing Factors in Cultural Adjustment."
            Missiology, Vol. 2, No. 1

Dye, Sally Folger
    1974   "Decreasing Fatigue and Illness in Field-Work."
            Missiology, Vol. 2, No. 1.

Eliade, Mircen
    1976   *Witchcraft, Occultism and Cultural Fashions.*
            Chicago: University of Chicago Press.

Engel, James F.
    1980   *Contemporary Christian Communication: Its Theory
            and Practice* Nashville: Thomas Nelson.

Engel, James F. and Norton, H. Wilbert
    1975   *What's Gone Wrong With the Harvest*? Grand Rapids:
            Zondervan Publishing House.

Engel, James F., Kornfield, W.J., and Oliver, V.L.
    1974   "What's Gone Wrong With Our Harvesting?"
            Missiology, Vol. 2, No. 3.

Erny, Ed
    1979   "That's The Trouble With You Missionaries - A
            Short Story." *Evangelical Missions Quarterly*,
            Vol. 15, No. 2.

Flatt, Donald
    1973   "The Cross-Cultural Interpretation of Religion
            in Africa." *Missiology*, Vol. 1, No. 3.

Foster, George A.
    1962   *Traditional Culture and Technological Change.*
            New York: Harper & Row.

Franklin, Karl J.
    1979   "Interpreting Values Cross-Culturally." *Missiology*, Vol. 7, No. 3.

Frizen, Edwin L., Jr.
1972   "Executives Tell Mission Profs What They Think."
            Evangelical Missions Quarterly, Vol. 8, No. 2.

Glasser, A. F.; Hiebert, P. G.; Wagner, C. P.; and Winter,
    1976   R. D. *Crucial Dimensions in World Evangelization*,
            Pasadena, CA: William Carey Library.

Glasser, Arthur F.
    1978   "Missiology -- What's It All About?" *Missiology*,
            Vol. 6, No. 1

1978   "Reflections on Training for Mission." *Missi-
        ology*, Vol. 6, No. 2.

1966   "Critical Look at the Wheaton Congress from Five
        Perspectives." *Evangelical Missions Quarterly*,
        Vol. 3, No. 1.

Glover, Robert Hall,
    1946   *The Bible Basis of Missions*. Chicago: Moody Press.

Goldschmidt, Walter
    1966   *Comparative Functionalism*. Berkley, CA: Univer-
            sity of California.

Gordon, Milton
    1964   *Assimilation in American Life*. New York: Oxford
            University Press.

Goving, Paul
    1975   "New Shape of Colombia Demands Sensitive Mission-
            aries." *Evangelical Missions Quarterly*, Vol. 2,
            No. 3.

Grunlan, Steve, and Mayers, Marvin K.
    1979   *Cultural Anthropology: A Christian Perspective*.
            Grand Rapids: Zondervan Publishing House.

Gilliland, Dean S.
    1973   "The Indigenous Concept in Africa." *Missiology*,
            Vol. 1, No. 3.

Herndon, Helen L.
    1980   "How Many 'Dropouts' Really are 'Pushouts'?"
            Evangelical Missions Quarterly, Vol. 16, No. 1.

Herskovits, Melville
    1964   *Cultural Dynamics*. New York: Alfred Knopf

Hesselgrave, David
    1978   *Theology and Mission*. (ed.), Grand Rapids: Baker
            Book House.

    1978   "Dimensions of Crosscultural Communication."
            Readings in Missionary Anthropology II. Edited
            by William A. Smalley, Pasadena, CA: Wm. Carey
            Library.

1978   *Communicating Christ Cross-Culturally*.   Grand Rapids: Zondervan Publishing House.

1975   "The Missionary of Tomorrow--Identity Crisis Extraordinary." *Missiology*, Vol. 3, No. 2

Hickman, John M.
1978   "Linguistics and Sociocultural Barriers to Communication." *Readings in Missionary Anthropology*. Edited by William A. Smalley, Pasadena, CA: Wm. Carey Library.

Hiebert, Paul G.
1976   *Cultural Anthropology*.   Philadelphia: J. B. Lippincott.

1978   "Missions and Anthropology: A Love/Hate Relationship." *Missiology*, Vol. 6, No. 2.

1978   "Introduction: Mission and Anthropology." *Readings in Missionary Anthropology*. Edited by William A. Smalley, Pasadena, CA: William Carey Library.

Hile, Pat
1977   "Communicating the Gospel in Terms of Felt Needs." *Missiology*, Vol. 6, No. 4.

Hoebel, E. Adamson
1972   *Anthropology: The Study of Man*.   New York: McGraw-Hill Book Company

Isaias, Juan
1966   *The Other Side of the Coin*.   Grand Rapids: Wm. B. Eerdmans.

Kane, J. Herbert
1974   *Understanding Missions*.   Grand Rapids: Baker Book House.

1975   *The Making of a Missionary*.   Grand Rapids: Baker Book House.

1974   "Changes in Missiological Studies." *Evangelical Missions Quarterly*, Vol. 10, No. 1

1973   *Winds of Change in the Christian Mission*.   Chicago: Moody Press.

1976   *Christian Missions in Biblical Perspective*.
        Grand Rapids: Baker Book House.

1981   *The Christian World Mission: Today and Tomorrow*.
        Grand Rapids: Baker Book House.

Kearney, Michael
    1975   "Worldview Theory and Study." *Annual Review of Anthropology*, Vol. 4.

Keesing, Roger M. and Keesing, Felix M.
    1971   *New Perspectives in Cultural Anthropology*. New York: Holt, Rinehart and Winston, Inc.

Kelly, David C.
    1978   "Cross-Cultural Communication and Ethics." *Missiology*, Vol. 6, No. 3.

Kornfield, David
    1979   "What It Costs to Prepare." *Evangelical Missions Quarterly*, Vol. 15, No. 3.

Kraft, Charles H.
    1973   "Dynamic Equivalence Churches." *Missiology*, Vol. 1, No. 1.

    1973   "The Incarnation, Cross-Cultural Communication and Communication Theory." *Evangelical Missions Quarterly*, Vol. 9, No. 4.

    1974   "Ideological Factors in Intercultural Communication." *Missiology*, Vol. 2, No. 3.

    1977   "Can Anthropological Insight Assist Evangelical Theology?" *Christian Scholar's Review*, Vol. 7, Nos. 2 and 3.

    1978   "Christian Conversion or Cultural Conversion." *Readings in Missionary Anthropology*. Edited by William A. Smalley, Pasadena, CA: Wm. Carey Library.

    1978   "An Anthropological Apologetic for the Homogeneous Unit Principle." *Occasional Bulletin of Missionary Research*, Vol. 2, No. 4.

    1979   *Communicating the Gospel God's Way*. Ashland, Ohio: Ashland Theological Seminary.

1979   *Christianity in Culture*. Maryknoll, NY: Orbis
        Books.

1980   Syllabus Notes for Intercultural Communication
        class. School of World Mission, Fuller Theolog-
        ical Seminary.

Kraft, Marguerite G.
1978   *Worldview and the Communication of the Gospel*.
        Pasadena, CA: Wm. Carey Library.

Ladd, George Eldon
1956   *The Blessed Hope*. Grand Rapids: Wm. B. Eerdmans
        Publishing Co.

Larson, Donald N. and Smalley, William A.
1972   "Becoming Bilingual: Guide to Language Learning."
        Pasadena, CA: William Carey Library.

Larson, Donald N.
1978   "The Visible Missionary: Learner, Trader, Story
        Teller." *Missiology*, Vol. 6, No. 2.

1977   "Missionary Preparation: Confronting the Presup-
        positional Barrier." *Missiology*, Vol. 5, No. 1.

1966   "Cultural Static and Religious Communication."
        Evangelical Missions Quarterly, Vol. 3, No. 1.

Lindsell, Harold
1970   *An Evangelical Theology of Missions*. Grand
        Rapids: Zondervan Publishing House.

Loewen, Jacob A.
1975   *Culture and Human Values: Christian Intervention
        in Anthropological Perspective*. Pasadena, CA:
        Wm. Carey Library.

Luzbetak, Louis
1963   *The Church and Cultures*. Techny, IL: Word Pub-
        lishing.

McCurry, Don M.
1976   "Culture Change and Its Relation to Literacy."
        Missiology, Vol. 4, No. 3.

McGavran, Donald A.
1955   *How Churches Grow*. New York: Friendship House.

1970   *Understanding Church Growth*. Grand Rapids: Wm.
        B. Eerdmans Publishing Company.

1972   *Crucial Issues in Missions Tomorrow*. (ed.),
        Chicago: Moody Press.

1974   *The Clash Between Christianity and Cultures*.
        Washington: Canon Press.

1980   *Understanding Church Growth*. (revised), Grand
        Rapids: Wm. B. Eerdmans Publishing Company.

1979   *Ethnic Realities and the Church*. Pasadena: Wm.
        Carey Library.

Malefijt, Annemarie deWaal
1977   *Images of Man: A History of Anthropological
        Thought*. New York: Alfred A. Knopf.

Malinowski, Bronislaw
1945   *The Dynamics of Culture Change*. New Haven: Yale
        University Press.

Martin, Alvin
1974   *The Means of World Evangelization: Missiological
        Education at the Fuller School of World Mission*.
        (ed.), Pasadena, CA: Wm. Carey Library.

Mayers, Marvin K.
1974   *Christianity Confronts Culture*. Grand Rapids:
        Zondervan Publishing House.

1974   *Biculturalism Evangelism: Philippine Focus*.
        Pasadena, CA: Wm. Carey Library.

1974   "The Filipino Samaritan: A Parable of Responsible
        Cross-Cultural Behavior." *Missiology*, Vol. 6,
        No. 4.

Mostert, John
1968   *The Preparation of a Missionary*. Wheaton, IL:
        Accrediting Association of Bible Colleges.

Nida, Eugene A.
1954   *Customs and Culture*. New York: Harper & Row.

1960   *Message and Mission*. New York: Harper & Row.

1968   *Religion Across Cultures.* New York: Harper & Row.

1974   *Understanding Latin Americans.* Pasadena, CA: Wm.
         Carey Library.

1978   "The Role of Cultural Anthropology in Christian
         Missions." *Readings in Missionary Anthropology.*
         Edited by William A. Smalley, Pasadena, CA: Wm.
         Carey Library.

1978   "New Religions for Old: A Study of Culture Change."
         Readings in Missionary Anthropology. Edited by
         William A. Smalley, Pasadena, CA: Wm. Carey
         Library.

Niebuhr, Helmut Richard
1956   *Christ and Culture.* New York: Harper & Row.

Parshall, Philip
1979   "God's Communicator in the 80's." *Evangelical
         Missions Quarterly*, Vol. 15, No. 4.

Pencille, William R.
1975   "Summer Missionaries--Are They Worth It?" *Evan-
         gelical Missions Quarterly*, Vol. 11, No. 4.

Pentecost, Edward C.
1974   *Reaching the Unreached.* Pasadena, CA: Wm. Carey
         Library.

Peters, George W.
1965   "Training Missionaries for Today's World." *Evan-
         gelical Missions Quarterly*, Vol. 2, No. 1.

1971   "Missionary of the 70's." *Evangelical Missions
         Quarterly*, Vol. 7, No. 2.

1972   *A Biblical Theology of Missions.* Chicago: Moody
         Press.

Redfield, Robert
1953   "Primitive Worldview and Civilization." *The
         Primitive World and Its Transformation.* Ithica,
         NY: Cornell University Press.

Reyburn, William D.
    1978   "Identification in the Missionary Task." *Readings in Missionary Anthropology*. Edited by William A. Smalley, Pasadena, CA: Wm. Carey Library.

    1978   "Polygamy, Economy and Christianity in the Eastern Cameroun." *Readings in Missionary Anthropology*. Edited by William A. Smalley, Pasadena, CA: Wm Carey Library.

    1978   "The Message of the Old Testament and the African Church." *Readings in Missionary Anthropology*. Edited by William A. Smalley, Pasadena, CA: Wm. Carey Library.

    1978   "The Missionary and Cultural Diffusion." *Readings in Missionary Anthropology*. Edited by William A. Smalley, Pasadena, CA: Wm. Carey Library.

Richardson, Don
    1974   *Peace Child*. Glendale, CA: Regal Books.

Roundhill, Kenneth S.
    1976   "The Adjustment Required of a Missionary in Japan." *Evangelical Missions Quarterly*. Vol. 12, No. 1.

Satterwhite, James P.
    1966   "Learn to Cope with Stress." *Evangelical Missions Quarterly*, Vol. 2, No. 1.

Schaller, Lyle E.
    1972   *The Change Agent*. Nashville: Abingdon Press.

Schwartz, Glenn
    1973   *An American Directory of Schools and Colleges Offering Missionary Courses*. Pasadena, CA: Wm. Carey Library.

Shank, David A.
    1979   "The Problem of Christian Cross-Cultural Communication Illustrated: Research Notes on 'The Finding of the Prophet Harris' by M. Benoit, September 1926." *Missiology*, Vol. 7, No. 2.

Shenk, Joseph C.
    1973   "The Missionary Identification and Servanthood." *Missiology*, Vol. 1, No. 4.

Shenk, Wilbert
    1973   "Theology and the Missionary Task." *Missiology*,
            Vol. 1, No. 3.

Simpson, David Stewart
    1978   *A Philosophy of Missiological Education.* Un-
            published Doctor of Missiology dissertation,
            School of World Mission, Fuller Theological
            Seminary.

Smalley, William A. (ed.)
    1978   *Readings in Missionary Anthropology.* Pasadena,
            CA: Wm. Carey Library.

    1978   "Culture Shock and the Shock of Self-Discovery."
            Readings in Missionary Anthropology. Pasadena,
            CA: Wm. Carey Library

    1978   "Respect and Ethnocentrism." *Readings in Mis-
            sionary Anthropology.* Pasadena, CA: Wm. Carey
            Library.

Starr, Timothy
    1978   *Church Planting: Always in Season.* Canada: no
            publisher.

Stewart, James C.
    1971   *American Cultural Patterns: A Cross-Cultural
            Perspective.* La Grange Park, IL: Intercultural
            Network, Inc.

Stringham, James A.
    1970   "Likely Causes of Emotional Difficulties Among
            Missionaries." *Evangelical Missions Quarterly*,
            Vol. 6, No. 4.

Taber, Charles R.
    1970   "What About a Lifetime Commitment?" *Evangelical
            Missions Quarterly*, Vol. 7, No. 1.

Taylor, Robert B.
    1973   *Introduction to Cultural Anthropology.* Boston:
            Allyn & Bacon, Inc.

Tippett, Alan R.
    1968   "Anthropology: Luxury or Necessity?" *Evangel-
            ical Missions Quarterly*, Vol. 1, No. 5.

1971   *People Movemevts in Southern Polynesia,* Chicago:
        Moody Press.

1973   "Anthropology and Post-Colonial Mission Through
        a China Filter." *Missiology*, Vol. 1, No. 4.

1973   *Verdict Theology in Mission Theory.* Pasadena,
        CA: Wm. Carey Library.

1977   "Conversion as a Dynamic Process in Christian
        Mission." *Missiology*, Vol. 5, No. 2.

Troutman, Charles H.
1966   "What Really Keeps Students from Volunteering for
        Missions?" *Evangelical Missions Quarterly*, Vol.
        2, No. 3.

Voget, Fred W.
1975   *A History of Ethnology.* New York: Holt, Rine-
        hart and Winston.

Wagner, C. Peter
1971   *Frontiers in Mission Strategy.* Chicago: Moody
        Press.

1972   *Church/Mission Tensions Today.* (ed.) Chicago:
        Moody Press.

1974   *Stop the World, I Want To Get On!* Glendale, CA:
        Regal Books.

1975   "Missionaries and Missions Can 'Salt the Soup'
        Too Much." *Evangelical Missions Quarterly*, Vol.
        11, No. 3.

1979   *Our Kind of People.* Nashville: Knox Press.

1983   *On the Crest of the Wave.* Ventura, CA: Regal
        Books.

Wagner, C. Peter and Dayton, Edward R.
1981   *Unreached Peoples '81.* Elgin, IL: David C.
        Cook Publishing Company.

Wakatama, Pius
1976   *Independence for the Third World Church.* Downer's
        Grove, IL: InterVarsity Press.

Wambutda, Daniel N.
    1978   "An African Christian Looks at Christian Mis-
            sions in Africa." *Readings in Missionary Anthro-
            pology*, Edited by William A. Smalley, Pasadena,
            CA: Wm. Carey Library.

Whiteman, Darrell L.
    1974   "The Christian Mission and Culture Change in New
            Guinea." *Missiology*, Vol. 2, No. 1.

Winter, Ralph D.
    1974   "The Two Structures of God's Redemptive Mission."
            Missiology, Vol. 2, No. 1.

Winter, Ralph D. and Hawthorne, Steven
    1981   *Perspectives On the World Christian Movement: A
            Reader*. Pasadena, CA: William Carey Library.

Wong, James, et. al.
    1973   *Missions From the Third World*. Singapore: Church
            Growth Center.

Index

Acculturation, 56
Advocate, 124
Agent of Change, 128, 129, 142
Ambassadors of Christ, 3
Ancestor worship, 105
Animism, 100, 101, 107, 111,
    120
Ascension of Christ, 171–172,
    178

Banks, Donald, 88–89
Barnett, Homer, 123, 124, 131
    132
Barney, Linwood, 62, 72
Behavioral sciences, 2, 8, 27
Bible translation, 138–141
Biblical imperatives, 1, 2
Biblical-theological dimen-
    sions, 163
Biculturalism, xi, xii, 143–
    146, 155, 157, 161, 181,
    183
Blanchard, Wendell, 105
Bock, Philip K., 21, 38, 39,
    122, 123
Body language, 73, 74
Bonding, 63 ff.

Brewster, Thomas, and Brewster,
    Elizabeth, 59, 60, 62, 64–
    65, 66–67, 68, 69, 83, 107,
    110
Bride price, 94
Bryant, David, 149–150
Buddhism, 111–112, 133

Change: incentives for, 121–122
    resistance to, 120–121
    stability and, 122–123
Church, 2, 142, 156 ff., 175,
    181, 184–185
Church age, 176
Church growth, 47, 55–56, 185
Contextualization, 138–139, 142
Conversion, 132, 135, 138
Cook, Harold, 5
Cross-cultural training, 7, 8,
    10–11, 26, 27, 74, 130, 143,
    155, 156, 181, 184
Crucifixion, 168
Cultural anthropology, xi, 8–10,
    26–31, 35, 83, 116
Cultural awareness, 27, 28, 83
Cultural baggage, 145, 146
Cultural barriers, 30, 85, 88,
    110, 112, 116

Cultural cues, 90, 92
Cultural divergence, 13, 17, 18, 30, 111, 114
Cultural relativism, 22, 23, 30
Cultural stress, 84
Culture, 13-16, 17, 81-82, 96 107, 112, 129, 130, 138, 144
Culture change, 119 ff., 128-129, 131, 132, 138, 139, 142
Culture learning, 79, 85, 89, 96, 97
Culture shock, 79 ff., 96-97

Dayton, Edward R., 50, 157-158
Deer, Donald, 75-76
Demographic factors, 20
Disease theory, 101, 106-107
Dubose, Francis M., 164
Dye, T. Wayne, 84
Dynamic equivalence: translations, 139-141; churches, 141-142, 156-161, 184

E-1, E-2, E-3, 157-158
Ecological factors, 19
Effective ministry, 146
Eliade, Mircen, 105-106
Ellul, Jacques, 57
Emic/Etic approaches, 28
Enculturation, 15
Engel, James, 135-138, 140, 142
Engel scale, 135-138
Ethclass model, 49-52
Ethnic groups, 51, 156
Ethnocentrism, 13, 21-24, 86-88, 183, 184
Evangelism, 51, 157, 158, 183
Event-orientation, 105
Extended family, 41

Flatt, Donald, 113
Fluency, 75 ff.
Form and meaning, 93-96

Formal equivalence churches, 159
Frizen, Jack, 27
Functional equivalents, 91-92
Functionalism, 16, 129

Glasser, Arthur F., 10
Glover, Robert Hall, 171
God's casebook, 139, 140
God's purposes, 2
Gordon, Milton, 49
Government service, 156
Graham, D. Bruce, 148-149
Great Commission, 2, 33, 136, 148, 170, 171, 172, 175, 184, 186
Group decision-making, 41-45, 47, 133
Grunlan and Mayers, 5, 9, 16, 30, 36-37, 73, 74, 75, 79

Hall, E.T., 106
Herskovits, Melville, 121-122
Hesselgrave, David, 46, 57, 72-73, 74, 103-104, 112
Hickman, John, 63
Hidden peoples, 49-51
Hiebert, Paul G., 8-9, 15, 16, 20, 21, 23-24, 29-30, 37, 39, 73-74, 93, 102, 103, 106, 114, 125, 144-145
Hinduism, 111-112
Hoebel, E. Adamson, 13, 15, 17, 19, 38, 39, 40, 41
Holy Spirit, viii, ix, 9, 131-132, 139, 145, 146, 151, 158, 161, 171-175, 183, 185, 186
Homogeneous Unit Principle, 47 ff., 52
Hutterites, 17, 125

Inadequate preparation, 4
Incarnation, 167
Innovation, 123-128, 142; basic stages in, 125; risks with, 125-126; accep-

tance and rejection of, 126-128

Intercultural communication, 21, 30, 31, 35-36, 59, 64, 74-75, 79, 85-86, 92, 97, 102, 103, 114-115, 134, 143-144, 146, 181-182

Isolation, 20-21, 67-68

Kane, J. Herbert, 1, 9, 151, 153-154, 164, 174, 178

Kearney, Michael, 99

Keesing, Roger M., 14, 18, 23, 112, 139

Kinesics, 73-75

Kinship relationships, 40 ff., 58

Kluckhorn, Florence, 14, 104

Kraft, Charles, 107-111, 114, 123, 124, 139-142, 159, 160, 161

Kraft, Marguerite, 100, 101, 103, 109

Ladd, George Eldon, 179

Language learning, 59, 69-70, 75, 77-78, 85-86, 102, 182

Language school, 66 ff.

Larson, Donald, 4, 60, 61-62, 63, 65, 67, 69, 71, 81, 82, 84, 86-87, 90, 102

Lausanne Committee, 49, 157, 158-160

Liefeld, Walter L., 44

Living Bible, The, 141

Loewen, Jacob, 39

Luzbetak, Louis, 7, 10, 80, 88

McGavran, Donald A., 34-35, 42, 43-44, 46, 47, 48, 53, 54, 55, 56-57, 58

Malinowski, Bronislaw, 16, 129

Mayers, Marvin K., 8, 22, 24, 26, 74, 89, 90, 91, 92, 93, 95, 96, 110, 129, 130, 145-147

Mimicry, 70-71

Missiological studies, 185-186

Missionary dropouts, xi, 184

Monocultural approach, 4, 7, 143-144, 157

Motivation, 61

Multi-individual conversion, 43

Mutual respect, 24, 26, 52, 111, 146

New Testament and missions, 166 ff.

Nida, Eugene A., 9, 28, 30, 33, 35-36, 46, 57-58, 61, 70, 71, 76-77, 78, 87, 94, 111-112, 113, 114-115, 116, 119-120, 138

Nigeria, 19, 160-161

Nonverbal communication, 72 ff.

Northern Thai, 100-101

Norton, H. Wilbert, 135-136

Nuclear family, 41

Oberg, Kalervo, 81, 83

Old Testament and missions, 164-166

Paul, the Apostle, 2, 158-159, 185

Peace Corps, 155

Pentecost, 173-174

Pentecost, Edward, 57

People-movement, 134

Phillips' translation, 141

Phonetics, 71

Pike, Kenneth, 28

Polygamy, 131

Preparation of missionaries, xi, 1, 5, 11, 25, 31, 59, 79, 129, 143 ff., 181-186

Purpose and scope, xi, xii

Race, 19

Radcliffe-Brown, A.R., 16, 129

Receptor people, 5

Redfield, Robert, 45

Redfield's continuum, 45

Religion, 49, 50, 113, 133

Resistance-receptivity axis, 54-55

Resurrection of Christ, 169
Return of Christ, 177–179
Reyburn, William, 120, 121
Richardson, Don, 114

Sawi people, 114
Schaller, Lyle, 125–126, 138–139
Schwartz, Glenn, 6–7
Short term missions, 151 ff.;
    evaluation of, 153
Smalley, William A., 9, 21,
    24, 25, 31, 60, 81, 82,
    83, 84, 86, 87, 90
Social class, 37
Social structures, 33 ff., 47,
    50, 57
Society, 17
Soil testing, 52–53, 54
Sogaard, Viggo, 136
Space perception, 105–106
Spiritual preparation, 6, 163
Status and role, 36 ff., 57
Subculture, 16–17
Summer missions, 151–153, 156
Survivals, 96
Symbols, nature of, 112
Symbolism, 95–96, 112 ff.
System, 16, 103–104, 129–130,
    139, 146

Taylor, J. Hudson, 10

Taylor, Robert, 13, 17, 19, 21,
    23, 37, 45, 121, 126–128,
    130
Thailand, vii, 18, 53, 100–101,
    105, 106, 120
Theory of natural groupings,
    110, 111
Third World missions, xii, 183
Time orientation, 88–89, 104–105
Tippett, Alan R., 11, 27, 29,
    42, 43, 128, 132, 133–135
Tools of relationship, 89 ff.,
    97
Tradition, 119, 120

Urban/rural factors, 45

Wagner, C. Peter, 47, 48, 49–50,
    51–52, 147, 157–158, 177
Whiteman, Darrell, 129, 131
Winter, Ralph, 51, 148, 157, 164
Witness, 174
World, xi, 6, 10, 11, 13 ff.,
    186
World Christian, 147–151
Worldview, 99 ff., 107–112, 113–114, 116–117, 139–140, 182
Worldview barriers, 110–111, 116
Worldview functions, 107

Yoruba, 19

LYMAN E. REED, D.Miss., is Professor of Bible and Missions at Briercrest Bible College, Caronport, Saskatchewan, where he has taught for over 12 years. He and his wife, Dorothy, served with Overseas Missionary Fellowship in North Thailand for 12 years doing pioneer evangelism and church planting. He received his BA from Columbia Bible College, his MA from Wheaton Graduate School, and his Doctor of Missiology from the School of World Missions, Fuller Theological Seminary.

Books by the William Carey Library

General

American Missions in Bicentennial Perspective edited by R.
Pierce Beaver, $10.95, paper, 448 pp.

The Baha'i Faith: Its History and Teachings by William McElwee
Miller, $10.95, paper, 444 pp.

The Birth of Missions in America by Charles L. Chaney, $7.95,
paper, 352 pp.

By Ones and By Twos: Single and Double Missionaries by Jean-
nie Lockerbie, $4.95, paper, 96 pp.

Dr. Sa'eed of Iran by Jay M. Rasooli and Cady Allen, $6.95,
paper, 190 pp.

*Education of Missionaries' Children: The Neglected Dimension
of World Mission* by D. Bruce Lockerbie, $2.95, paper, 76 pp.

An Evangelical Agenda: 1984 and Beyond, The Billy Graham
Center, $5.95, paper 234 pp.

Frederick Franson: Model for Worldwide Frontier Evangelism,
by Edvard P. Torjesen, $4.95, paper, 124 pp.

The Life and Times of an MK by C. John Buffam, $9.95, paper,
208 pp.

The Missionary Family by Betty Jo Kenney, $5.95 paper, 112 pp.

Missionary Kid--MK by Edward Danielson, $5.95 paper, 92 pp.

The Night Cometh: Two Wealthy Evangelicals Face the Nation
by Rebekah Winter, $2.95 paper, 96 pp.

Not In Vain: The Story of North Africa Mission by Francis R.
Steele, $4.95 paper, 192 pp.

A People for His Name: A Church-Based Mission Strategy by
Paul A. Beals, $9.95x paper, 234 pp.

Student Mission Power: Student Volunteer Movement for Missions
$6.95 paper, 248 pp.

200 Rooms In the Inn: The Story of Providence Mission Homes
by Mercedes Gribble with Hope Friedmann, $3.95 paper, 112 pp.

Mission Strategy and Theology

Blessing in Mosque and Mission by Larry Lenning, $5.95 paper,
172 pp.

Challenge and Crisis in Missionary Medicine by David J. Seel,
$3.95 paper, 160 pp.

Chinese Theology in Construction by Wing-hung Lam, $11.95x
paper, 320 pp.

Christ and Caesar in Christian Missions edited by Edwin J.
Frizen, Jr. and Wade T. Coggins, $5.95 paper, 160 pp.

Church Growth and Group Conversion by Donald McGavran et al.,
$3.95 paper, 128 pp.

Committed Communities: Fresh Streams for World Missions by
Charles J. Mellis, $5.95 paper, 160 pp.

Contextualization of Theology: An Evangelical Assessment by
Bruce C.E. Fleming, $5.95 paper, 148 pp.

Everything You Need to Grow a Messianic Synagogue by Phillip
E. Goble, $3.95 paper, 176 pp.

Everything You Need to Grow a Messianic Yeshiva by Phillip E.
Goble, $10.95 paper, 298 pp.

Here's How: Health Education by Extension by Ronald and Edith
Seaton, $3.45 paper, 144 pp.

The Indigeneous Church and the Missionary by Melvin L. Hodges,
$2.95 paper, 108 pp.

*The Last Age of Missions: A Survey of 3rd World Mission
Societies* by Lawrence Keyes, $10.95 paper, 238 pp.

Literacy, Bible Reading, and Church Growth Through the Ages
by Morris G. Watkins, $5.95 paper, 240 pp.

Mission Theology 1948-1975: Years of Worldwide Creative Tension by Rodger C. Bassham, $10.95 paper, 456 pp.

Perspectives on the World Christian Movement: A Reader, Ralph
D. Winter and Steven C. Hawthorne, editors, $14.95x paper,
$19.95x hardback, 850 pp.

Preparing Missionaries for Intercultural Communication by
Lyman E. Reed, $6.95x paper, 208 pp.

Reaching the Arabs: A Felt Need Approach by Timothy Matheny,
$7.95x paper, 264 pp.

Reaching Our Generation, Wade T. Coggins and Edwin Frizen,
editors, $5.95 paper; 132 pp.

Readings in Dynamic Indigeneity, Charles H. Kraft and Tom N.
Wisley, editors, $12.95x paper, 584 pp.

Readings in Third World Missions, Marlin L. Nelson, editor,
$6.95x paper, 304 pp.

Seeds of Promise: World Conference on Frontier Mission
Allan Starling, editor, $8.95 paper, 258 pp.

*Social Context and Proclamation: A Socio-cognitive Study in
Proclaiming the Gospel Cross-culturally* by David Filbeck,
$8.95x paper, 132 pp.

The Stranger Who Is Among You by James Duren & Rod Wilson,
$2.95 paper, 80 pp.

*Unto the Uttermost: Missions in the Christian Churches/Churches
of Christ*, Doug Priest Jr., editor, $8.95x paper, 313 pp.

Area and Case Studies

Aspects of Pacific Ethnohistory by Alan R. Tippett, $5.95
paper, 216 pp.

A Century of Growth: The Kachin Baptist Church of Burma by
Herman Tegenfeldt, $10.95 cloth, 540 pp.

A Christian Approach to Muslims: Reflections From West Africa
by James P. Dretke, $3.95 paper, 288 pp.

The Church in Africa, 1977, Charles R. Taber, editor, $6.95
paper, 244 pp.

Church Growth in Burundi by Donald Hohensee, $4.95 paper,
160 pp.

Church Growth in Japan by Tetsunao Yamamori, $4.95 paper,
184 pp.

Church Planting in Uganda: A Comparative Study by Gailyn Van
Rheenen, $4.95 paper, 192 pp.

The Cross and the Floating Dragon: The Gospel in the Ryukus
by Edward Bollinger, $10.95 paper, 348 pp.

Ethnic Realities and the Church: Lessons from India by Donald
A. McGavran, $8.95 paper, 272 pp.

The Growth of Japanese Churches in Brazil by John Mizuki,
$8.95 paper, 240 pp.

Indonesian Revival: Why Two Million Came to Christ by Avery
T. Willis, Jr., $6.95 paper, 288 pp.

Melanesians and Missionaries by Darrell Whiteman, $15.95x
paper, 560 pp.

Missions Growth: A Case Study on Finnish Free Foreign Mis-
sion by Lauri Ahonen, $5.95 paper, 72 pp.

People Movements in the Punjab by Frederick and Margaret Stock,
$8.95 paper, 388 pp.

A People Reborn by Christian Keysser, $9.95x paper, 306 pp.

The Protestant Movement in Bolivia by C. Peter Wagner, $3.95
paper, 262 pp.

The Religious Dimension in Hispanic Los Angeles by Clifton
L. Holland, $10.95 paper, 550 pp.

The Role of the Faith Mission: A Brazilian Case Study by Fred
Edwards, $3.45 paper, 176 pp.

Siam Then: The Foreign Colony in Bangkok by William Bradley,
$8.95 paper, 207 pp.

Toward Continuous Mission: Strategizing for the Evangeliza-
tion of Bolivia by Douglas Smith, Jr., $4.95 paper, 208 pp.

Understanding Latin Americans: With Special Reference to
Religious Values and Movements by Eugene Nida, $5.95 paper,
176 pp.

The Unresponsive: Resistant or Neglected? by David C.E. Liao,
$5.95 paper, 168 pp.

Worldview and the Communication of the Gospel: A Nigerian
Case Study by Marguerite G. Kraft, $7.95 paper, 240 pp.

Applied Anthropology

The Church and Cultures: Applied Anthropology for the Relig-
ious Worker by Louis J. Luzbetak, $7.95x paper, 448 pp.

Communicating the Gospel God's Way by Charles Kraft, $2.95x
paper, 64 pp.

Customs and Cultures: Anthropology for Christian Missions
by Eugene Nida, $6.95x paper, 322 pp.

Manual of Articulatory Phonetics by William A. Smalley,
$12.95x paper, 522 pp.

Oral Communication of the Scripture: Insights from African
Oral Art by Herbert Klem, $9.95x paper, 256 pp.

Readings in Missionary Anthropology II, William A. Smalley,
editor, $13.95x paper, 912 pp.

Tips on Taping: Language Recording in the Social Sciences
by Wayne and Lonna Dickerson, $4.95x paper, 208 pp.